CLIA Final Rules for Quality Systems

Quality Assessment Issues and Answers

James O. Westgard, PhD, FACB
Sharon S. Ehrmeyer, PhD, MT(ASCP)
Teresa P. Darcy, MD, MMM, FASCP, FCAP

Westgard QC, Inc.
7614 Gray Fox Trail
Madison WI 53717
Phone 608-833-4718 Fax 608-833-0640 http://www.westgard.com

Westgard QC

Library of Congress Control Number: 2004106160
ISBN 1-886958-20-3
Published by Westgard QC
7614 Gray Fox Trail
Madison, WI 53717

Phone 608-833-4718

First Word

It is a distinct pleasure and honor to have the "first word" when dealing with the authors of this book. In the 1960's Jim and I were graduate students in analytical chemistry with Professor Walter Blaedel at the University of Wisconsin and have now been colleagues at UW for more than 35 years. Sharon has been a friend and colleague for more than 30 years. More recently we have welcomed Teresa into the clinical laboratory team at Wisconsin. With that perspective I would like to offer the reader these first words.

CLIA is finally final, but that doesn't mean the discussions, interpretations and arguments are over. With adoption of the January 2003 Final Rule and the publication in January 2004 of the 300+ page Appendix C of the State Operations Manual, or "the interpretive guidelines" as they are commonly called, we gain insight into the government's plans for the implementation of the Final Rule. They focus on ***quality assessment*** which is a combination of quality control and quality assurance – the terms used in the original CLIA'88 regulations.

From a historical perspective, in the 1960's clinical laboratories were struggling with such profound questions as "What is a standard?" and "What is a control?" By then Deming and Juran had convinced the world that it was not just quality control (number crunching) but a total systems approach that is needed to achieve total "Quality." In the 1950's starting with Shewhart's concepts, Levey and Jennings demonstrated the application of statistical QC as a fundamental "Quality tool" in clinical laboratories. By 1981 Jim had published the seminal papers on what would become the "Westgard Rules," the statistical basis for one of today's quality tools for ongoing assessment of laboratory testing processes.

The authors of this book help all of us take the next step. They point out how the CLIA regulations can be applied in laboratories to assure the quality of test results. Sharon has coined the phrase "From quality assurance to assured quality." This is a gigantic step for all today's "partners" — laboratory scientists, manufacturers and regulators. It means, for each, going beyond the letter of the law and doing what is right based on rigorous scientific principles and profound (in the Deming sense) understanding of the testing process. It is the complete antithesis of assuming that minimum regulatory compliance is a substitute for true Quality practices. To take the next step, all of the partners must look beyond the minimum requirements of the regulations and adopt the tools of true Quality practices.

This book goes well beyond what might be expected from the title. The most important contribution is the introduction and application of Six Sigma concepts and methodology to provide quantitative metrics and guidance for method validation and intra-laboratory QC. The Six Sigma approach provides a universal methodology for the full, integrated quality assessment of any laboratory process, including the pre-analytic, analytic, and post-analytic components. Given that the emphasis in the Final Rule is with quality assessment of the complete testing process, including pre and post analytical processes, the Six

Sigma methodology presented here is a new and better approach than current QA practices. In my opinion it also opens the door to the possibility, perhaps the methodology, of a full collaborative partnership involving regulators, laboratory scientists and manufacturers. With this effort, Jim, Sharon and Teresa have offered the opportunity to move the reader from CLIA'88 (application of a minimum set of statistical rules for QC) to CLIA 2003 and into the 21st century (development of a true quality assessment system).

Perhaps the most controversial issue addressed here is the recent recommendation for "equivalent QC procedures," in short, the proposed reduction of daily QC to weekly or monthly QC for certain instruments having "internal procedural controls." The protocol for adoption of equivalent QC, as spelled out in the State Operations Manual, is a 10, 30 or 60 day assessment of performance using internal and conventional external controls to determine the adequacy of using the internal controls only. Here's a good example where the use of Sigma-metrics provides a much better assessment of method performance and a more informed judgment on the suitability of equivalent QC procedures.

As the "elder" statesman of this Wisconsin group (admittedly only by a narrow margin over Jim), it gives me great pleasure to recommend this book to serious laboratory scientists, manufacturers, and regulators. As we move into the era of implementing the Final CLIA Rule, we have an opportunity to adopt an enlightened approach for true Quality practices.

Ronald R. Laessig, PhD
Director, Wisconsin State Lab of Hygiene
Madison, Wisconsin

Acknowledgments

We're very appreciative of Ron Laessig's willingness to write the Foreword to this book. Ron understands the roles of the regulator as well as the regulatee. We tend to identify most strongly with the regulatee and sometimes need to be reminded that the regulator really does have honorable intentions.

Being government employees, we do understand that some jobs are more difficult than others, and some are completely thankless – such as those of the regulators, inspectors, and accreditors. We appreciate the willingness of people in government agencies and professional accreditation organizations to talk with us about many of the issues discussed in this book. We often found they have the many of the same concerns, but have a very limited range of options and approaches to address those concerns. We sincerely thank them for their help, particularly Judy Yost, Cecelia Hinkel, Rhonda Whalen, Nancy Yeransian, Joanne Born, and Kathleen Steffens.

As with all the books published by Westgard QC, it is Sten Westgard who makes it possible. In this case, time was of the essence in getting these materials together and in proper form for fast publication. Sten got it done right on time while juggling many other professional and family responsibilities. We know that Henry and Maren were at his feet, on his lap, or in his arms often while this book was being completed.

James O. Westgard, PhD, FACB
Madison Wisconsin

About the authors

James O. Westgard, PhD, FACB, is a Professor in the Department of Pathology and Laboratory Medicine at the University of Wisconsin Medical School, where he teaches in the Clinical Laboratory Science program. He is also Faculty Director of Quality Management Services at the Clinical Laboratories, University of Wisconsin Hospital & Clinics, and President of Westgard QC, Inc.

Sharon S. Ehrmeyer, PhD, MT(ASCP), is a Professor in the Department of Pathology and Laboratory Medicine and Director of the Clinical Laboratory Sciences Program at the University of Wisconsin Medical School. She is a member of JCAHO's Professional and Technical Advisory Committee for its Laboratory Accreditation program and is Regulatory Affairs editor for Point of Care, the journal of near-patient testing and technology.

Teresa P. Darcy, MD, MMM, FASCP, FCAP is the Medical Director of the Clinical Laboratories at the University of Wisconsin Hospital and Clinics and is an Associate Professor at the Department of Pathology and Laboratory Medicine at the University of Wisconsin Medical School. Dr. Darcy received her Master in Medical Management degree from the University of Southern California Marshall School of Business.

Publisher's Note:

I have spent more than 25 years of my career advocating the improvement of quality control in the healthcare laboratory. During that time, I've discovered that it's not enough to talk about the need for quality improvement; people need tools and techniques to make improvements. So I developed statistical tools to help identify poor quality control practices and I also developed planning processes to guide quality improvements. Then I discovered it wasn't enough to demonstrate those quality improvement tools; people needed these tools to be practical, fast, and easy to use. So I collaborated with others on the creation of software that automated the tools and techniques and provided a simple, graphic interface for users. Even then, I discovered that having the theory and tools and software wasn't enough; people need a quick and convenient way to learn and access these things. So I started publishing books, offering online courses, and posting articles on the Internet.

At some points in this book, you'll see that I mention Westgard QC products. You may be tempted to say this book is therefore commercially biased. I admit to several biases: I am biased against the "status quo" compliance mentality of current QC practices in healthcare. I am biased against the idea that we should abandon statistical QC for unproven, less capable QC techniques. I am biased against the short-sighted, short-term impulse to slash costs in every area of healthcare laboratories and eliminate any investment in quality control. These very biases, and my unwillingness to accept the decline of quality control practices, led me to found a company that would create products to enable and enhance the improvement of quality control.

I'm happy to admit that I'm proud of every book that has been published by Westgard QC and that I'm proud of all the software we've released. In the text, where possible, I note some of the other products available on the market that provide the same quality improvement tools or techniques. In some cases, however, there is no other software or book out there on the market – for instance, our software may remain the only software in the world that provides automatic QC selection for quite some time. I look forward to the day when future editions of this book will list some competitors.

Table of Contents

1: CLIA and Quality Systems

The CLIA Final Rule published in January 2003 [1] brings to the end a series of revisions that have covered a period of over ten years. Remember, we are still talking about the implementation of Clinical Laboratory Improvement Amendments, known as CLIA-88 because the law was passed back in 1988. The "rules" for implementing CLIA-88 have only now been finalized after years and years of comments and revisions. This is actually the final, final, final, final, final CLIA Rule!

A copy of the changes included in the Final CLIA Rule can be printed from the Internet by going to the following URL: http://www.phppo.cdc.gov/clia/regs2/toc.asp. Look for the link "Requirements Relating to Quality Systems and Certain Personnel Qualifications (2003)" that appears in the paragraph at the top of the page. That page also includes a table of contents for the entire CLIA Rule, incorporating the final language for all sections from the many final drafts that have been published. If you want a complete paper copy, be prepared to print for hours!

The Final Rule appeared in the January 24, 2003 issue of the Federal Register on pages 3640 through 3714. These pages include an extensive "crosswalk" table (9 pages) to help you locate the requirements in the reorganized document, comments and responses that led to the final rule (23 pages), a summary of changes (4 pages), estimates of financial impact (22 pages), and the Final Rule itself (13 pages). Out of 54 pages, the thirteen pages from 3702 to 3714 contain what is new and different in the Final Rule. Read the other materials if you have time and want some insight into why changes were made.

A new focus on Quality Systems

The Final Rule contains a number of changes that will have a significant impact on quality management practices in laboratories. It focuses on "quality systems," a new term that first shows up in this latest revision of the rules. To promote the concept of quality systems, CMS has developed a new logo that identifies the following key components:

- General laboratory systems
- Pre-analytic systems
- Analytic systems
- Post-analytic systems

The idea is that all of these components are important for assuring the quality of laboratory testing services. All of these components must be managed, monitored, and improved. In the CLIA Final Rule, the process of assuring the quality of laboratory testing is called quality assessment, rather than quality assurance or quality management, as it was called in earlier revisions.

Regardless of the terminology chosen, the intent of the Final Rule is to promote the development, implementation, delivery, monitoring, and improvement of high quality laboratory services. This requires an effective quality management system. In that context, it seems appropriate to begin this discussion with definitions of terms to facilitate the reading and understanding of the regulations.

CMS, HCFA, NCCLS, ISO

The Final Rule was developed by the Centers for Medicare and Medicaid Services (CMS), formerly known as the HealthCare Finance Agency (HCFA). They drew heavily on a document "A Quality System Model for Health Care" [2] that was published by the National Committee for Clinical Laboratory Standards (NCCLS). The definitions of many of the important terms in the NCCLS document are taken from other documents developed by the International Standards Organization (ISO). Note that NCCLS is also undergoing a name change and may be known as the Clinical and Laboratory Standards Institute (CLSI) or the Healthcare Testing Standards Institute (HTSI) by the time you read this. If you find the changing names interesting and/or confusing, you'll have even more fun with the changing terminology in the CLIA Final Rule.

Quality laboratory service

Let's start with definitions of some basic terms and concepts in quality management and quality systems [2]:

- ***Quality.*** The totality of characteristics of an entity that bear on its ability to satisfy stated and implied needs.
- ***Service.*** The result generated by activities at the interface between the provider and the customer and by provider internal activities to meet the customer needs.
- ***Customer.*** The recipient of a product or service provided by the supplier.
- ***Supplier.*** An organization that provides a product or service to the customer.

In this context, the quality of laboratory services depends on many characteristics, such as painless acquisition of a specimen, quick turnaround time for the test, correctness of the test result, proper documentation and reporting, and reasonable cost. The actual requirements for these different characteristics are set by both internal and external customers. For example, physicians are internal customers, whereas patients are the external customers. The physicians usually set clinical requirements for performance characteristics such as analytical quality and turnaround time, whereas the needs of patients dictate requirements related to comfort and convenience, such as quick and painless specimen acquisition. Reimbursements for services are often dictated by other customers – the insurer or the government payer. As part of paying for services, the government requires compliance with the CLIA regulations, thus the government is a customer who has requirements that must be satisfied by the laboratory. And we all know that money talks, so the government is an important customer who insists on certain levels of quality in laboratory services.

Procedures, processes, and systems

Continuing with definitions from NCCLS and ISO [2]:

- ***Procedure.*** A specified way to perform an activity.
- ***Process.*** One or more interrelated resources and/or activities that transform inputs (e.g., intent, policies) into outputs (eg., instruction, procedures).
- ***Quality system.*** The organizational structure, resources, processes, and procedures needed to implement quality management.

Given that a procedure is a specified way of performing one activity, a process can be considered a combination of procedures. The detailed descriptions of procedures and processes define the way work gets done in the laboratory. A ***system*** can be considered to be an even bigger combination of activities, procedures, and processes.

It is a fundamental principle of quality management that problems with quality are predominantly caused by problems with processes, not problems with people. If something can go wrong, it will! Work processes need to be designed, developed, and improved so things can't go wrong. That means the laboratory must properly manage all of its processes for acquiring and preparing specimens, analyzing specimens, and reporting test results.

Total testing process and laboratory quality system

These terms have a somewhat special application in the CLIA regulations and build on the general concepts of processes and systems. For example, the processes for acquiring specimens, analyzing specimens, and reporting test results are part of the total analytical system shown in the accompanying figure. Process A is pre-analytic, B is analytic, and C is post-analytic. The combination of these processes was previously called the "Total Testing Process" in earlier versions of the CLIA Rules, but is now considered to be part of the "quality system," so you will have to adapt to the terminology found in different documents.

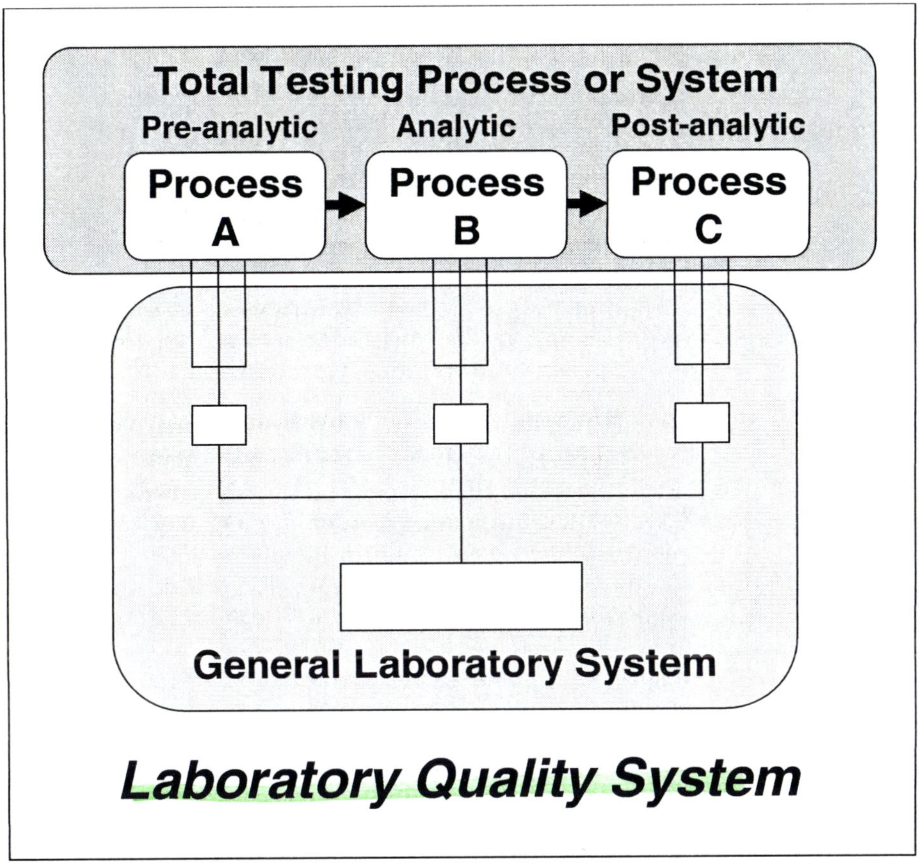

All the people who operate, supervise, manage, and direct these processes are part of the general laboratory system, which includes processes for hiring and training, acquiring appropriate resources, such as space, equipment and supplies, etc., and very importantly, processes for managing all those resources effectively. The CLIA rules for personnel, resources, and facilities apply here. We prefer to think of the organization as a support structure, rather than a top-down control structure, because it demonstrates the important role of bench-level analysts in producing quality services, as well as the important role of management to provide the resources necessary to deliver quality services.

Management commitment is critical to quality because managers are invested with the power to change and improve processes. If processes are main cause of most problems, it is necessary to make changes to processes to improve quality. Those changes may require more training of the analysts, new and better analytical systems, better supplies and equipment, more optimal staffing, etc. Management has the responsibility to make those changes, therefore management must be involved and actively support quality.

Bringing all of these people and processes together gives us the Laboratory Quality System, which includes everything that is important for providing laboratory testing services that will meet the needs of our patients!

A quality management process

Implicit in the laboratory quality system are all the management activities that are defined in the NCCLS/ISO terms:

- ***Quality management.*** All activities of the overall management function that determine quality policy objectives and responsibilities; and implement them by means such as quality planning, quality control, quality assurance, and quality improvement within the quality system.
- ***Quality assurance.*** Planned and systematic activities to provide adequate confidence that requirements for quality will be met.

Note that quality management includes quality planning, quality control, and quality assurance, and that quality assurance emphasizes that "requirements for quality will be met." These have been identified as important components of a laboratory quality management process described in the scientific literature [3,4], as shown in the accompanying figure.

The terms in the figure are defined as follows [5]:

- ***QLP, Quality laboratory processes.*** The policies, procedures, personnel standards, and physical resources that determine how the work gets done in the laboratory.

- ***QC, Quality control.*** Procedures for monitoring the work processes, detecting problems, and making corrections prior to delivery of products or services.

- ***QA, Quality assessment.*** Monitoring the totality of features and characteristics of quality that bear on the achievement and satisfaction of customer needs.

- ***QI, Quality improvement.*** Activities aimed at determining the causes or sources of problems identified by QC and QA and implementing improvements that eliminate these problems.

- ***QP, Quality planning.*** Activities concerned with establishing, validating, and verifying that testing services meet customer needs.

- ***Quality goals.*** Statements, definitions, and policies that describe the quality that must be achieved to satisfy customer needs and regulatory requirements.

This figure emphasizes the connections between the components to provide a feedback loop centered on quality goals, which apply to all of the components and drive the quality management process. The feedback loop shows the dynamic nature of the process and how the components work together to provide for the continuous improvement of quality. Quality assurance is the outcome of the quality management process, rather than a component of that process. The end result is to assure that the quality of laboratory testing services meets customer needs, as well as regulatory requirements.

Validation and verification

The quantitative management of quality requires that performance be assessed and compared to the implied needs of customers and the defined requirements of regulators and/or accreditors. This aspect of assessing conformance to needs and requirements is described as validation and verification in NCCLS/ISO terms [2].

- ***Validation.*** Action [or process] of proving that a procedure, process, system, equipment, or method used works as expected and achieves the intended result.
- ***Verification.*** The confirmation by examination and provision of objective evidence that specified requirements have been fulfilled.

In the CLIA Final Rule, the term ***quality assessment*** is used to broadly encompass the concepts and practices of validation and verification, as well as related terms such as evaluation, audit, etc. Quality assessment should involve sound scientific methodology and data analysis (statistics) to provide an objective comparison of the measured or observed performance to the defined quality goals and requirements.

Compliance vs quality and excellence

The term "compliance" is best understood as meaning "not in disagreement with government regulations." That term may also be applied to accreditation guidelines from inspection organizations that are deemed to have standards at least as demanding as CLIA. "Deemed" organizations, such as the College of American Pathologists

(CAP), the Joint Commission for Accreditation of Healthcare Organizations (JCAHO), and the Commission for Office Laboratory Accreditation (COLA), actually provide most of the inspection of laboratories for compliance to the CLIA rules. In practice, compliance mainly affirms agreement with the letter of the law, not necessarily the spirit of the law. Compliance does not guarantee quality!

Unfortunately, compliance and quality represent quite different attitudes and approaches. The "compliancy mentality" is to satisfy the minimum requirements necessary to get by, whereas the "quality mentality" is to achieve all the goals and requirements for excellent service. Compliance generally means achieving minimum performance, or at best, average performance, whereas quality means achieving excellent performance.

The conflict in the approaches for compliance and quality create a dilemma for laboratories. They must be in compliance with CLIA regulations, but that by itself doesn't mean the services provided meet the needs of the customers. CLIA does not *prevent* a laboratory from achieving excellence; in fact, many of the CLIA rules point laboratories in the right direction for achieving excellence. However, CLIA doesn't *require* that laboratories achieve excellence because there are easy ways to come into compliance without doing the hard work of achieving excellence.

Our focus on quality assessment

The most significant changes in the Final Rule have to do with quality assessment, particularly method validation and quality control practices. For that reason, we have chosen to focus this book on quality assessment issues. Most of this book attempts to provide practical answers in those areas. We cover other aspects of the Final Rule in less detail, such as personnel requirements and method complexity classifications, pre and post-analytic processes, and the program changes in accreditation and inspection. There are many other literature resources available to deal with other aspects of CLIA, such as the *Poor Man's Guide to the Regulations* [6], and it is not our intent to duplicate their coverage. Our intent is to help you with the latest issues emerging from the latest "final" draft of the CLIA regulations.

References

1. US Centers for Medicare & Medicaid Services (CMS). Medicare, Medicaid, and CLIA Programs: Laboratory Requirements Relating to quality Systems and Certain Personnel Qualifications. Final Rule. Fed Regist Jan 24 2003;16:3640-3714.

2. NCCLS. A quality system model for health care: Approved guideline, NCCLS Document GP26-A. NCCLS, 940 West Valley Road, Suite 1400, Wayne, PA 190087-1898 USA 1999.

3. Westgard JO, Burnett RW, Bowers GN. Quality management science in clinical chemistry: a dynamic framework for continuous improvement of quality. Clin Chem 1990;36:1712-1716.

4. Westgard JO, Barry PL, Tomar RH. Implementing total quality management (TQM) in healthcare laboratories. CLMR 1991;5:353-370.

5. Westgard JO. Basic Planning for Quality. Madison, WI:Westgard QC, Inc., 2000, pp 15-18.

6. Laessig RH, Ehrmeyer SS. The New Poor Man's (Person's) Guide to the Regulations (CLIA-88, JCAHO, CAP & COLA). Madison, WI:R&S Consultants, 2003.

2: Key Changes in CLIA Final Rule

This discussion will focus on key changes in the Final Rule in organization, terminology, and regulations that will have major impact [1]. Later discussions will get into more detail about specific parts of the Final Rule and ideas on how to address and implement those provisions.

Key changes in organization and terminology

For a complete and detailed list of all the changes, refer to pages 3674 to 3678 of the January 24 2003 Federal Register [1]. The key changes are:

- ***Organization follows the flow of a patient specimen through the laboratory***, i.e., pre-analytical, analytical, and post-analytical systems. This reorganization has been hyped as a big change to make the document consistent with a "quality systems" approach, as described in the NCCLS GP26-A2 document [2]. It's not such a big deal since there are only two columns for "Pre-analytical Systems" [section 493.1240, page 3705-6] and one paragraph for "Post-analytic Systems Assessment" [section 493.1299, page 3713], with 8 pages in-between for "Analytic Systems." Most of the Final Rule focuses on the quality of the analytic phase and there is much more detail in this area than in the pre- and post-analytic areas.
- ***"Non-waived Testing" replaces High and Moderate Complexity.*** Because of the large increase in the number of test methods that have been classified as "waived" testing, the methods remaining tend to be only those of high complexity, thus the original classifications of moderate complexity and high complexity are now lumped together under the classification of "non-waived testing." This is actually the organizational change that contributes to simplification of the Final Rule. No more switching back and forth between high and moderate complexity due to different requirements – it's just one set of requirements for non-waived tests – *except for personnel, where the distinction between moderate and high*

complexity tests still affects the qualifications for personnel performing those tests.

- ***QA now means quality assessment rather than assurance.*** This change is supposed to focus the quality effort on assessment of performance in all phases of the testing process and also place new importance on establishing and following written polices and procedures, taking corrective action, and making changes in policies and procedures to prevent problems from reoccurring. In our view, assessment actually leads to assurance when coupled with these steps to make corrective actions permanent by changes in policies and procedures that prevent problems from occurring in the future. This change in terminology adds little to the understanding of quality management and the quality improvement process, but you need to be aware of it anyway. If the inspector asks about your quality assessment procedures, you need to recognize the new terminology. Everything that was formerly quality assurance is now part of the quality assessment section on analytic systems.

- ***Definitions added for calibration, calibration verification, FDA-cleared or approved test system, reportable range, and test system.*** Evidently there has been so much confusion about the exact meaning of these terms that new definitions have been added to the Final Rule. See page 3702. These clarifications may be driven, in part, by CAP's use of different terms for analytical measurement range (AMR) and clinically reportable range (CRR). There are a lot of questions about this and we will take up some of the specific issues in Chapter 8.

Key changes in regulations

- ***NONE FOR WAIVED TESTING!***

- ***Final Rule became effective April 24, 2003.*** All laboratories must now meet and follow the QC requirements as of April 24, 2003.

- ***Laboratories must validate the performance of all methods introduced after April 24, 2003.*** For unmodified FDA-cleared or approved systems, this includes the following performance characteristics: accuracy, precision, reportable range, and reference intervals (normal values). For modified or non FDA-cleared systems, additional characteristics include analytical sensitivity, analytical specificity and interference, reference intervals, and another performance characteristics required for the test (such as detection limit). CAP has consistently required validation of all methods, so if you're a CAP-approved laboratory you've been doing this all along. JCAHO has been a little more selective, but basically if you're JCAHO-approved, you've also been doing this. The main impact will be on small labs that up until now have only been following the manufacturer's directions, have a procedure manual, analyze two controls per day, and document corrective actions.

- ***Laboratories must determine calibration and control procedures for new methods.*** This requirement is found in section 493.1253 (3) on page 3707. To our knowledge, this is a new statement that appears for the first time in this Final Rule. It is explained as follows: "The laboratory must determine the test system's calibration procedures and control procedures based upon the performance specifications verified or established." The reason for this is probably due to the two items below – the lack of FDA clearance of QC instructions and the transfer of QC responsibility to laboratories.

- ***FDA clearance of manufacturer's QC instructions has been eliminated.*** This is the part of the original CLIA rule that has been postponed and postponed and postponed and postponed. At long last, they have just killed it because of the government's inability to implement the process. FDA clearance of QC was a key feature in CLIA because it provided the basis for allowing laboratories to follow the manufacturer's directions for QC. If those QC directions were sound, then the laboratory should be able to produce quality results. If not sound, there would be no guarantee that quality will be okay. The responsibility for quality now rests with the laboratory because the manufacturer's directions will not be validated by FDA.

- ***Laboratories are responsible for having control procedures that monitor the complete analytical process, take into account the performance specifications of the method, detect immediate errors, and monitor long-term precision and accuracy.*** This is where the responsibility for QC has been reassigned to the laboratory because the manufacturer and FDA are now off the hook. The laboratory and the laboratory director are now responsible for doing the right QC right. This change in responsibility is actually good because neither the FDA nor the manufacturer are able to determine what QC is right in your laboratory. Only you can do that, based on the quality needed for your patient population, the performance observed for the method as operated by the people in your laboratory, and the QC procedures that you are able to implement in your laboratory. The regulations don't provide any guidance on how to do that, but we describe a practical approach in Chapter 14.

- ***Minimum QC now two levels per day rather than per run.*** In the absence of doing what is required in the item above, the default requirement is a minimum of two levels of control per day. Note the change from per run to per day in the Final Rule. This really isn't such a big change since a run was earlier defined as being a maximum of 24 hours and many laboratories already equate a run with a 24 hour period. There are some additional details that apply to certain kinds of tests, e.g., blood gases where the requirement is still one control every eight hours or one control each time specimens are tested unless automatic instrumentation internally verifies calibration at least every 30 minutes (see specialty areas on pages 3708-3712).

- ***Reductions in QC requirements in specialty and subspecialty areas.*** In general, the amount of QC has also been reduced in many (but not all) of the standards for specialty areas (pages 3708-3712). These changes to reduce the amount of QC are the basis for claiming the Final Rule reduces the financial burden of QC. This will receive a lot of attention because it shows the government's willingness and interest in containing the cost of laboratory testing. For example, the standard for control procedures in hematology now reads "one control material must be tested each 8 hours of operation," whereas two were required before the Final Rule. Remember, if the manufacturer's requirements for QC are more than CLIA, the laboratory must follow the manufacturer's requirements. Before reducing QC, laboratories should consider the implications of the requirements to "detect immediate errors" and "monitor over time the accuracy and precision of test performance that may be influenced by changes in test system performance and variance in operator performance." These two requirements precede the specialty requirements and still must be satisfied.

- ***Proficiency Testing (PT) grading requirement for 80% agreement has been restored.*** This has to do with the grading of PT surveys. In the past, the criterion for consensus agreement has been 90%, meaning that 90% of laboratories must be in agreement before a test can be graded. Because many PT samples were not getting graded when the 90% criterion was applied, a non-graded sample actually benefited the laboratory (was as good as getting an answer that was correct within the PT criterion for acceptable performance). By lowering the grading criterion to 80%, more PT samples will now be graded.

- ***Non-PT'd tests must have accuracy verified by the laboratory.*** Any tests performed by the laboratory, but not included in a PT program, must have their accuracy verified by the laboratory at least twice per year. This is not really new, but is being restated more clearly. It means the laboratory will need to define some procedure to periodically compare performance on patient specimens over time, compare performance with another laboratory, compare performance with a reference laboratory, or test reference materials that have known or assigned values.

- ***Laboratory director qualifications for high complexity testing clarified and implemented as of February 24, 2003.*** This affects laboratories that formerly performed the high complexity tests that are now part of non-waived testing.

The laboratory director must hold an earned doctoral degree in a chemical, physical, or biological, or clinical laboratory science from an accredited institution and be certified by a board approved by HHS. Alternative qualifications include 2 years of laboratory training or experience and 2 years of laboratory experience directing or supervising high complexity testing prior to February 24, 2003.

Other changes

In addition to the changes above, here are some of the fine details of other changes in the Final Rule, as summarized in the December 2003 issue of Clinical Laboratory News [3].

General laboratory system

- A lab director's signature on new or revised procedures must be obtained prior to implementation of that procedure.
- Labs must have mechanisms in place to verify the accuracy of its patient-specific and calculated data.
- Records of the test system performance specifications that are established and verified by the laboratory must be kept for the lifetime of the test system or a minimum of 2 years.
- Once a state removes a lab's license and revokes the right to operate within a state due to non-compliance with the state's licensure requirements, CMS can now coordinate with the state and take an action to revoke a lab's CLIA certificate.
- Labs that cease operations must retain all records for the specified timeframes in the regulations.
- Records, slides, blocks, and tissue must be maintained and stored in a manner that ensures proper preservation, and the laboratory must arrange a secure area for storage that will ensure proper preservations of specimens and records.
- A facility that provides transfusion services must report transfusion reactions to laboratories and federal and state authorities.

- For molecular test procedures, there must be separate areas for specimen preparation, amplification, and product detection, and for reagent preparation.
- Molecular amplification procedures that are not in closed systems must now have a unidirectional workflow.
- Written lab safety procedures must now only be accessible – they no longer must be posted.

Pre-analytic system

- Oral test requests or telephone orders are acceptable, provided that the laboratory solicits a written or electronic authorization within thirty days of the oral request.
- Specimen source, when appropriate, should be solicited on the test request.
- If the lab transcribes or enters test requisition or authorization information into a record system or laboratory information system, the laboratory must have an ongoing mechanism to ensure the accuracy of manual entry.
- Labs must document the date and time a specimen is received.
- Specimens may only be referred for testing to a CLIA-certified lab.

Analytic system

- Labs must document the steps they take to identify, correct, and prevent the recurrence of problems.
- All improvement actions need to be documented and communicated to all staff.

Post-analytic system

- Patient test data must now be correlated with sex, age, and clinical data.
- Test reports should now include the unit of measurement or interpretation or both.

Still some confusion!

It might be considered a good measure of a regulatory document that the end result is some confusion. That leaves room for interpretation and flexibility in the implementation of the Final Rule. CMS has indicated they will use the State Operations Manual (SOM) [4] to provide guidance to both the laboratories and the inspectors on how to implement the rules. Here are some of the areas where it will be important to refer to the SOM:

- ***Do laboratories need to gear up to validate new methods?*** Yes, that appears to be the major impact of the Final Rule for many small laboratories that have been inspected for compliance to CLIA, rather than inspected for CAP or JCAHO accreditation. Any laboratory that performs non-waived testing will have to perform validation studies for any new methods introduced after April 24, 2003. The SOM provides further clarifications of the experimental procedures that will be expected by the inspectors.

- ***Can laboratories just run two controls per day and get by?*** Probably! In spite of the language that implies the need for control procedures to detect immediate errors and monitor the long-term precision and accuracy of the method, a simple default remains – just run two controls per day.

- ***Can laboratories deviate from the practice of running two controls per day?*** Yes, that is possible. You can always run more QC, which is often needed. And under the SOM guidelines for "equivalent QC procedures," there are options to run less QC. However, we think it is dangerous to reduce the already minimal daily QC to weekly or even monthly QC, as we will explain in Chapter 13. In Chapter 14, we will describe the right way to select a QC procedure that is appropriate for the quality required by the test, the method performance specifications verified or established by the laboratory, and the control procedure's ability to detect immediate errors.

- ***Is Electronic QC still okay?*** We didn't think so until we saw the SOM and its description of "equivalent QC procedures." It looks like that was written to provide a way for Electronic QC to be used, as long as the laboratory runs external liquid controls weekly or monthly. CMS had a practical problem in that they had made a temporary allowance for Electronic QC, pending publication of the Final Rule. Now the Final Rule or the SOM has to deal with that issue. It's hard to see how Electronic QC fits the requirements of the Final Rule, particularly the standard 493.1256 that requires "having control procedures that monitor the accuracy and precision of the complete analytic process." The way out for Electronic QC is a later clause "unless CMS approves a procedure, specified in Appendix C of the State Operations Manual (CMS Pub. 7), that provides equivalent quality testing."

- ***What is "Equivalent QC"?*** CMS equates "equivalent quality testing" in the Final Rule to "equivalent QC procedures" in the SOM. The main effect of "equivalent QC" is to allow reduction of the frequency of running liquid controls from once a day, to once a week, or even to once a month, depending on the internal procedural controls provided by a manufacturer. This is one of the most controversial items in the CLIA Final Rule. The caveat in the SOM is that *"the director must consider the laboratory's clinical and legal responsibility for providing accurate and reliable patient test results versus the cost implications of reducing the quality control testing frequency."* **You can do this, but beware of your clinical and legal liability!**

- ***Can laboratories still follow the manufacturer's directions?*** Yes, you have to, but that doesn't eliminate the laboratory's responsibility to verify the manufacturer's performance claims. In addition, the lack of any specific directions on QC doesn't let the laboratory off the hook on QC. The laboratory should establish specific directions and, if conditions warrant, do more and better QC than recommended by the manufacturer. Also, if the manufacturer's QC directions require more QC than the minimum required by CLIA, the laboratory must follow the manufacturer's directions.

Regardless of the ambiguity in the regulations and the State Operations Manual, we recommend what is right and best for the laboratory and the patients you serve. Quality has to do with "doing the right thing right," which is our guiding principle and continues to be the best approach for defining quality management practices.

References

1.US Centers for Medicare & Medicaid Services (CMS). Medicare, Medicaid, and CLIA Programs: Laboratory Requirements Relating to quality Systems and Certain Personnel Qualifications. Final Rule. Fed Regist Jan 24 2003;16:3640-3714.

2. NCCLS. A quality system model for health care: Approved guideline, NCCLS Document GP26-A. NCCLS, 940 West Valley Road, Suite 1400, Wayne, PA 19087-1898 USA 1999.

3. Auxter-Parham S. CLIA guidelines to offer new QC options for labs: CMS introduces "equivalent" QC concept. Clin Lab News 2003;29(12):1,4,6.

4. CMS State Operations Manual – Interpretive Guidelines. Centers for Medicare and Medicaid Services. 2004

3: State Operations Manual and CMS Interpretive Guidelines

Most of us have questions about the meaning and interpretation of the CLIA rules and regulations. To address these issues, CMS has published **Interpretive Guidelines** that are available on the Internet [1, www.cms.gov/clia/appendc.asp]. Given that these guidelines were published on January 12, 2004, many of us also have questions about the meaning and interpretation of the new Interpretive Guidelines.

The Interpretive Guidelines are technically identified as Appendix C of the State Operations Manual (SOM, CMS Publication 7), a manual used by states in administering various federal programs, not just CLIA. However, these updated Interpretive Guidelines have a new twist in that they have become a companion to the final CLIA Rule [2]. In the past, surveyors primarily used the probes listed in the Guidelines during the inspection process to determine a laboratory's compliance with a particular standard. Now the document is being made available to laboratories to help them better understand the CLIA requirements and also to provide additional regulatory information not included in the Final Rule. For example, section §493.1256(d), Standard Control procedures, states: "Unless CMS approves a procedure, specified in Appendix C of the State Operations Manual, that provides 'equivalent quality testing,' the laboratory must..." follow the rules found in §493.1256 of the Federal Register [page 3707-8, reference 2]. The information on "equivalent quality testing" is found only in the SOM. Laboratories now need to utilize the SOM along with the CLIA regulations published in the Federal Register.

Organization

Appendix C includes 7 sections that are available as Portable Document Files (PDF) that can be downloaded to your computer or printed directly. The PDF format requires that you have the Adobe® Acrobat® Reader installed on your computer (which is available free and can be downloaded from the Adobe® website www.adobe.com/products/acrobat/readstep2.html.)

1. Policy for conducting surveys (270K PDF, 18 pages)
2. Index and Subparts A-H. General Provisions, Certificates and Proficiency Testing: §493.1100 – §493.865 (925K PDF, 59 pages)
3. Subpart J. Facility Administration: §493.1100 – §493.1105 (211K PDF, 11 pages)
4. Subpart K, Part 1. Quality System for Nonwaived Testing; General Laboratory systems, Preanalytic Systems & Analytic Systems - general requirements: §493.1200 – §493.1256 (770K PDF, 59 pages)
5. Subpart K, Part 2. Quality System for Nonwaived Testing; Analytic Systems – specialty and subspecialty requirements – and Postanalytic Systems: 493.1261 – 493.1495 (1.2MB PDF, 77 pages)
6. Subpart M. Personnel: §493.1351 – §493.1495 (585K PDF, 61 pages)
7. Subpart Q. Inspection: §493.1771 – §493.1780 (137K PDF, 11 pages)

All of this adds up to a total of 296 pages of new materials to help you better understand the CLIA Final Rule and how it will be applied in laboratory inspections.

Format and content

Unlike the previous Appendix C that was organized in table format, the new version follows the format:

Deficiency "D-tag number"
CLIA standard
Interpretive Guidelines, and Probes

In this book, we follow the SOM format and use the following conventions:

- **bold text (san serif font) restates the regulations**
- *and italics text (san serif font) restates the Interpretive Guidelines and Probes, as well as quotations from the Interpretive Guidelines of other organizations, such as CAP, JCAHO, or COLA.*

- Any other serif font text, *or in italics*, ***or in bold italics***, represents text written by the authors of this book.

Here's an example of the formatting for §493.1251(a) Standard: Procedure Manual.

D5401

§493.1251 Standard: Procedure Manual

(a) A written procedures manual for all tests, assays, and examinations performed by the laboratory must be available to, and followed by, laboratory personnel. Textbooks may supplement but not replace the laboratory's written procedures for testing or examining specimens.

Interpretive Guidelines §493.1251(a):

Procedures may be organized in the form of manuals, stored in computers and/or card files. Use D5401, if the procedure manual lacks any of the applicable information as specified in §493.1251(b)(1)-(14). If the laboratory has procedures that are not used for test performance, but are used for reference purposes, they may be placed in a reference section. You need not review reference procedures unless problems are identified with patient test results.

Centers for Disease Control and Prevention (CDC) and Armed Forces Institute of Pathology (AFIP) manuals, manufacturer's operating instructions, and package inserts, are acceptable provided the policies and procedures are available, and the methods in use are clearly indicated. If the laboratory modifies any procedure, the modification must be documented and verified/established as specified in §493.1253.

Probes §493.1251(a):

How does the laboratory ensure that personnel follow the procedures in the procedure manual? How are changes in procedures communicated to laboratory personnel? For competency issues, use D6030 or D6103 as applicable.

All CLIA standards have a "D-tag" assigned. When a laboratory is found in noncompliance with a particular standard, the surveyor cites the associated "D" number rather than the specific standard.

The *Interpretive Guidelines* section is designed to provide more information to both the laboratory and surveyor on how to meet the particular requirement. For the procedure manual example, the surveyor also is informed to use a specific D-tag "**D5410**" when the test site omits required information and to review the laboratory's reference procedures only when problems occur with patient test results.

The *Probes* section is included to assist the surveyor in determining whether the laboratory is in compliance with the standard. These probes are in the form of questions that the surveyor can ask to investigate how the laboratory ensures personnel follow the procedures and also to identify what mechanism is used to inform testing personnel of changes in the manual. Obviously, it is useful for the laboratory to be familiar with the probes since the surveyor may ask those exact questions during the inspection.

While there will be a D-tag for each CLIA standard listed, not all standards are included in the *Interpretive Guidelines* and/or *Probes* sections.

Issues and Answers

How should you use these Interpretive Guidelines if inspected by CMS?

If your laboratory is inspected for CLIA compliance, be very familiar with the guidelines and use them as a companion document to the Final Rule.

- The *Interpretive Guidelines* section will further clarify the intent of the standard and, perhaps, provide assistance on what documentation or what strategies should be included to meet the standard. With the procedure manual standard, the guidelines state that procedures may be organized in the form of manuals, stored in computers and/or card files.

- The *Interpretive Guidelines* are particularly important for further guidance on "equivalent quality testing," section §493.1256(d).
- The *Probes* provide some clues as to what the surveyor will want to find. Simply having a response to each probe can eliminate many potential inspection problems. For the procedure manual example, make sure mechanisms are in place to ensure that personnel follow the procedures and changes in the manual are communicated to laboratory personnel.

What if your laboratory is inspected by a professional accrediting organization?

- CMS "deems" or approves certain professional accrediting organizations, such as the College of American Pathologists (CAP), the Joint Commission for Accreditation of Healthcare Organizations (JCAHO), and COLA (formerly known as the Commission for Office Laboratory Accreditation), as having requirements as or more stringent than CLIA and therefore allows them to carry out laboratory inspections [3].
- Inspections conducted by these government-approved accrediting organizations are based on the specific testing requirements of the particular organization. By meeting the accrediting organization's requirements, test sites, in essence, also are meeting the CLIA requirements.
- In most cases, each of these organizations issues their own test standards and provides information similar to what appears in the *Interpretive Guidelines* section of Appendix C, for example:
  - ❍ CAP's Laboratory General Checklist item GEN.11742 asks [4]: *"Is there evidence that problems identified by proficiency testing and alternative performance assessment have been recognized and corrected?"*
    - § Under the COMMENTARY for this standard, the following clarification is provided: *"There must be evidence that the laboratory solves problems identified through proficiency testing and alternative performance*

assessment (as appropriate). Documentation of corrective/preventive action is required."

- JCAHO's standard QC.1.110 states [5]: *"The laboratory ensures that quality control results meet its criteria for acceptability before it reports patient test results."* The ELEMENTS OF PERFORMANCE section for this standard describes what the inspector will want to see: *(1) For each area of the laboratory, defined criteria exist for evaluating the acceptability of control and calibration results. (2) Individual results are not reported unless these criteria are met.*

Do the Interpretive Guidelines allow CLIA to change the rules published in the Federal Register?

That certainly appears to be the case. As we will discuss in Chapter 13, the *Interpretive Guidelines* for "equivalent quality testing" deviate greatly from the requirements for QC procedures stated in the Federal Register. The advantage of using the SOM to make these changes is that there is no need to solicit public comments on these changes and no need to formally defend those changes. In effect, the SOM gives CMS considerable flexibility in the way the CLIA rules are applied and enforced.

DO's and DON'Ts

- DO obtain a copy of Appendix C for access in your laboratory. You can decide whether to store that copy on your computer or to print a copy. One advantage of a printed copy is that its sheer size makes it evident there is a lot of direction being given to inspectors and should also make it obvious that the laboratory needs to pay attention to these materials.
- DO read the appropriate *Interpretive Guidelines* and *Probes* for clarification and guidance in addressing specific rules that you find critical or troublesome for your laboratory. The specific guidelines and probes given in the SOM should be helpful for formulating strategies, implementing plans, and preparing for inspection.

- DON'T be constrained or limited by the SOM. Recognize that the CLIA rules are *minimum* requirements for quality management. To assure quality test results for your patients, it may require doing more than the minimums specified by CLIA.
- DO what is right to manage quality – let that be the guiding principle, not the CLIA rules and the SOM *Interpretive Guidelines.*

References

1. Appendix C of SOM, Regulations and Interpretive Guidelines for Laboratories and Laboratory Services, http://www.cms.gov/clia/appendc.asp

2. CLIA Final Rule (2002 codification of all previous rules (1992-2002). http://www.phppo.cdc.gov/clia/pdf/42cfr49302.pdf and CLIA Final Rule (January 24, 2003) http://www.phppo.cdc.gov/clia/pdf/CMS-2226-F.pdf

3. Listing of government-approved accrediting organizations. http://www.cms.gov/clia/accrdorg.asp

4. CAP Laboratory Accreditation Checklists. http://www.cap.org/apps/docs/laboratory_accreditation/checklists/checklistftp.html

5. JCAHO standards. Joint Commission on Accreditation of Healthcare Organizations, One Renaissance Blvd., Oakbrook Terrace, IL 60181

4: Perplexity about Personnel and Complexity

The Final CLIA Rule did away with the use of the terms high complexity and moderate complexity and established one set of "quality assessment" standards for non-waived tests. Now instead of separate quality requirements for moderate and high complexity testing, there is only one set for non-waived testing. As a result, you may have the impression that there is only one set of personnel requirements for non-waived testing as well. NOT TRUE! Personnel qualifications still are related to test complexity, thus you have every right to be "perplexed" or confused.

Laboratories still need to meet the personnel requirements identified for moderate and high complexity testing. The only change in the Final Rule is for the director qualification in the high complexity category.

This discussion reviews the current personnel qualifications for testing under CLIA and identifies the appropriate sections in the CLIA regulations for each position. Details for each position, including specific responsibilities and requirements for directors in specialty and subspecialty areas, can be found in the most current codified edition, which contains all changes subsequent to the initial requirements identified in the February 28, 1992 Federal Register – see http://www.phppo.cdc.gov/clia/regs/toc.asp For the latest qualifications (01/24/03) for high complexity test director, see http://www.phppo.cdc.gov/clia/regs/toc.asp

General Requirements for Personnel

Waived Testing. For a laboratory performing only waived testing, there are no personnel requirements. These tests may be performed by anyone, although the Centers for Medicare and Medicaid Services (CMS) expect personnel to follow manufacturers' instructions and apply good laboratory practices.

Moderate and High Complexity Testing (Subpart M, §493.1403-1495). For a laboratory performing moderate complexity testing, qualified individual(s) need to be identified for four positions:

Director, Technical Consultant, Clinical Consultant, and Testing Personnel. High complexity testing requires that individual(s) be identified for five positions: Director, Technical Supervisor, Clinical Consultant, General Supervisor, Testing Personnel.

- Note that the position titles for each complexity level do not have to correspond to working titles used within the laboratory. The specific education and experience qualifications for each title vary according to the complexity of testing as well. A Medical Doctor (M.D.), Doctor of Osteopathy (D.O.), Doctor of Podiatric Medicine (D.P.M.), or Ph.D., with the appropriate experience can fill all the required positions for both complexity levels.

The Interpretive Guidelines (Appendix C of the State Operations Manual) available at http://www.cms.gov/clia/apcsubm.pdf are helpful in understanding each personnel category. The *Interpretive Guidelines and Probes* sections of Appendix C further clarify the educational and testing experience requirements and the responsibilities for individuals wanting to qualify for a specific personnel category and they identify what the surveyors are directed to investigate. Examples from the *Interpretive Guidelines and Probes* sections are included under the categories and identified by the "D-tag number" that corresponds to the specific CLIA personnel standard.

Moderate Complexity Testing Specific Personnel Categories and Qualifications

Director (§493.1403-1407): The director is responsible for all aspects of laboratory operation and administration. The director may delegate the duties to qualified individuals, but ultimately remains responsible for ensuring that all duties are properly performed. The director must be accessible, but is not required to be on-site when laboratory testing is performed. The director's qualifications range from a licensed doctor of medicine, osteopathy, or podiatry to an individual having a bachelor's degree in medical technology/clinical laboratory science or in the chemical, physical, or biological science. Each qualification requires specific training and/or experience in laboratory testing.

- *D6000 (§493.1403): The Condition: laboratory director is not met when the laboratory director:*
    - *– Position is not filled;*
    - *– Is not qualified; or*
    - *– Does not fulfill the laboratory director's responsibilities.*

    ❍ *An individual qualified as laboratory director may not qualify as a technical consultant in a particular specialty or subspecialty unless he or she has the required testing experience.*

- *D6004 (§493.1407 — Laboratory director responsibilities). If the laboratory has more than one person qualifying as director, the laboratory is required to designate one individual who has ultimate responsibility for overall operation and administration of the laboratory.*

    ❍ *The requirement that a laboratory must be under the direction of a qualified person is not automatically met simply because the director meets the education and experience requirements. It must be demonstrated that the individual is, in fact, providing effective direction over the operation of the laboratory.*

    ❍ *In determining whether the director responsibilities are met, consider deficiencies found in other conditions, e.g., facility administration, general laboratory systems, preanalytic systems, analytic systems, postanalytic systems, and proficiency testing.*

Technical Consultant (§493.1409-1413): The laboratory must employ one or more individuals who are qualified by education and either training or experience to provide technical consultation for each of the specialties and subspecialties of service in which the laboratory performs moderate complexity methods. The technical consultant establishes the quality standards of the laboratory through selecting and monitoring the laboratory's methods/instrumentation and evaluating and documenting the competency of the personnel. The technical consultant must be accessible, but is not required to be on-site when laboratory testing is performed. Qualifications for this position range from a licensed medical doctor or doctor of osteopathy certified in anatomic and/or clinical pathology to an individual having a bachelor's degree in medical technology/clinical laboratory science or in the chemical, physical, or biological science. Each qualification requires specific training and/or experience in laboratory testing.

- *D6036 (§493.1413): In a specialty in which neither the director nor testing personnel can qualify to provide technical consultation, the laboratory may engage the services of a qualified person either on a part-time or full-time basis for this service. Under these circumstances, the qualified person is not required to be on the premises full-time or at all times tests are being performed in his/her specialty(ies). However, the technical consultant must be available to provide consultation and should spend time in the laboratory sufficient to supervise the technical performance of the staff in his/her specialty(ies).*

Clinical Consultant (§493.1415-1419): The clinical consultant is the liaison between the laboratory and its customers. The "customers" consisting of both physicians who order tests and "lay" people, patients, who have full access to all medical records. This individual must be qualified to consult with and give opinions concerning the diagnosis, treatment, and management of patient care and be available to provide clinical consultation to the laboratory's clients. The clinical consultant is not required to be on-site when laboratory testing is performed. The clinical consultant must be a licensed medical doctor or doctor of osteopathy, doctor of podiatric medicine or individual having a doctorate in the chemical, physical, biological or clinical laboratory science and appropriate certification.

- *D6061 – Probe for §493.1419(c:) Has the clinical consultant reviewed the reports to ensure that test results include patient information required for specific patient interpretations?*

Testing Personnel (§493.1423-1425): Testing personnel are responsible for specimen processing, test performance, and reporting test results. For moderate complexity testing, personnel qualifications range from doctors of medicine, osteopathy or podiatry to an individual with a high school diploma or equivalent and specific, appropriate training/experience that includes having documented training prior to analyzing patient specimens.

- *D6074 - §493.1425(b)(5): If, during the survey, testing personnel demonstrate an inability to identify a problem that adversely affects a patient test result, cite D6029 under director responsibilities. Some examples of problems that may adversely affect patient test results may include, but are not limited to:*
  - *A pleural fluid that is mislabeled and, therefore, is processed as a urine culture;*
  - *Performing a potassium on a hemolyzed sample; or*
  - *Tests are incubated at 37°C when the manufacturer's instructions require 25°Cincubation.*

High Complexity Testing Specific Personnel Categories and Qualifications

Director (§493.1443-1445): The director is responsible for all aspects of laboratory operation and administration including the employment of personnel who are competent to perform test procedures, record and report test results promptly, accurately and proficiently, and for assuring compliance with the applicable regulations. The director may delegate the duties to qualified individuals, but remains responsible for ensuring that all duties are properly performed. The director must be accessible, but is not required to be on-site when laboratory testing is performed.

For high complexity testing, the director's qualifications include:

1. M.D., or D.O. with a current medical license in the state of the laboratory's location and certified in anatomic and/or clinical pathology by ABP or AOBP or equivalent qualifications;
2. M.D., D.O. or D.P.M. with a current medical license in the state the laboratory is located and one year laboratory training during medical residency;
3. M.D., D.O., or D.P.M. with current medical license in State of laboratory's location and 2 years experience in directing/ supervising high complexity testing;
4. Doctorate in chemical, physical, biological or clinical laboratory science and board certification;

5. Doctorate in a chemical, physical, biological, or clinical laboratory science from an accredited institution and serving as director of a laboratory performing high complexity testing (these individuals must also have two years of laboratory training or experience, or both; and two years of experience directing or supervising high complexity testing);
6. ON OR BEFORE 2/28/92 serving as a laboratory director and previously qualified or could have qualified as a laboratory director under laboratory regulations published March 14, 1990 (55 FR 9538);
7. ON OR BEFORE 2/28/92 qualified as director by the State in which the laboratory is located.

With the January 24, 2003 Final Rule, experienced directors without board certification, (5) above, will be "grandfathered." As of February 24, 2003, new doctoral degreed directors of high complexity testing will need board certification as identified in (4). The approved boards for both doctoral-degree directors and clinical consultants is available at: http://www.cms.gov/clia/dirclcon.asp.

- *D6077 — §493.1443: Section 353(i)(3) of the PHS Act states "No person who has owned or operated a laboratory which has had its certificate revoked may, within 2 years of the revocation of the certificate, own or operate a laboratory for which a certificate has been issued under this section." The term "State" as used in this provision, includes the District of Columbia, the Commonwealth of Puerto Rico, the Commonwealth of Northern Mariana Islands, the Virgin Islands, Guam and American Samoa.*

Technical Supervisor (§493.1447-1451): The laboratory must employ one or more individuals who are qualified by education and either training or experience to provide technical and scientific oversight for each of the specialties and subspecialties of service in which the laboratory performs high complexity tests or procedures. The technical supervisor establishes the quality standards of the laboratory through selecting and monitoring the laboratory's methods/instrumentation and evaluating and documenting the competency of the personnel. The technical supervisor must be accessible, but is not required to be on-site when laboratory testing is performed.

The technical supervisor's qualifications range from a licensed medical doctor or doctor of osteopathy certified in anatomic and/or clinical pathology to an individual having a bachelor's degree in medical technology/clinical laboratory science or in the chemical, physical, or biological science. Each qualification requires specific training and/or experience.

- *D6120—§493.1451(b)(7): In some instances, in-service training may be specifically related to an instrument or test, or may be very general in nature. The laboratory may establish its own format, content, and schedule or provide training on an as-needed basis. This is acceptable provided the laboratory does not have deficiencies related to test performance.*

- *D6120 — Probe for §493.1451(b)(8): What mechanism is used to ensure that testing personnel are following the laboratory's policies and procedures? When approved by the director, these policies and procedures may include manufacturer's instructions.*

Clinical Consultant (§493.1455-1457): The clinical consultant is the liaison between the laboratory and its customers. This individual must be qualified to consult with and give opinions concerning the diagnosis, treatment and management of patient care. The clinical consultant must be available to provide clinical consultation to the laboratory's clients, but is not required to be on-site when laboratory testing is performed. The qualifications for this position include only licensed medical doctors, doctors of osteopathy, doctors of podiatric medicine, and individuals having a doctorate in the chemical, physical, biological or clinical laboratory science and appropriate certification.

General Supervisor (§493.1459-1463): The laboratory must have one or more general supervisors who, under the direction of the laboratory director and supervision of the technical supervisor, provides day-to-day supervision of testing personnel and reporting of test results. In the absence of the director and technical supervisor, the general supervisor must be responsible for the proper performance of all laboratory procedures and reporting of test results. The general supervisor must be accessible (on-site) when laboratory testing is performed. The general supervisor's qualifications include:

1. Laboratory director of high complexity testing;
2. Technical supervisor of high complexity testing;
3. M.D., D.O. or D.P.M. with current medical license in the state where laboratory is located and 1 year training/experience in high complexity testing;
4. Doctorate in clinical laboratory science or chemical, physical or biological science and 1 year training/experience in high complexity testing;
5. Master's degree in clinical laboratory science, medical technology or chemical, physical or biological science and 1 year training/experience in high complexity testing;
6. Bachelor's degree in medical technology, or chemical, physical or biological science and 1 year training/experience in high complexity testing;
7. Associate degree in a laboratory science or medical laboratory technology and have at least 2 years of laboratory training or experience, or both, in high complexity testing;
8. Education and training equivalent to an associate degree in a laboratory science or medical laboratory technology and have at least 2 years of laboratory training or experience, or both, in high complexity testing: Education — 60 semester hours including either 24 semester hours of medical laboratory technology courses or 24 semester hours of science courses (6 hours of chemistry; 6 hours of biology; and 12 hours in chemistry, biology or medical laboratory technology, or any combination); and Training — either completion of an approved/accredited clinical laboratory or medical laboratory training program, which may be included in the 60 semester hours specified above or three months of documented laboratory training in each specialty in which the individual performs high complexity testing;
9. For blood gas analysis, earned an associate degree related to pulmonary function and have at least 2 years of laboratory training or experience, or both, in blood gas analysis;

10. On or before 2/28/92 qualified or could have qualified as a general supervisor under 42 CFR 493.1433 laboratory regulations published March 14, 1990 (55 FR 9538);

11. On or before 9/1/92, served as a general supervisor of high complexity testing and as of April 24, 1995, have at least 2 years of clinical laboratory training or experience, or both, in high complexity testing (either before or after completing the accredited or military medical laboratory training) and meet 1 of the following:

    1. Have graduated from an approved or accredited medical laboratory or clinical laboratory training program.

    2. Be a high school graduate or equivalent and have successfully completed at least a 50 week official U.S. military medical laboratory procedures course and have held the military enlisted occupational specialty of Medical Laboratory Specialist (Laboratory Technician).

12. On or before 9/1/92, served as a general supervisor of high complexity testing, and have high school diploma or the equivalent; and have at least 10 years of laboratory training or experience, or both, in high complexity testing, including at least 6 years of supervisory experience between 9/1/82 and 9/1/92.

- *D6164 — §493.1463: Interview several testing personnel to elicit information about the duties they perform and the degree of supervision they receive.*

Testing Personnel (§493.1487-1495): The testing personnel are responsible for specimen processing, test performance and for reporting test results. Qualifications for testing personnel include:

1. M.D., D.O., or D.P.M. with current medical license in the state where laboratory is located;

2. Doctorate in clinical laboratory science or chemical, physical or biological science;

3. Master's degree in medical technology, clinical laboratory science or chemical, physical or biological science;

4. Bachelor's degree in medical technology/clinical laboratory science or chemical, physical or biological science;

5. Associate degree in a laboratory science, or medical laboratory technology;

6. Education and training equivalent to an associate degree in a laboratory science, or medical laboratory technology: Education — 60 semester hours including either 24 semester hours of medical laboratory technology courses or 24 semester hours of science courses (6 hours of chemistry; 6 hours of biology; and 12 hours in chemistry, biology or medical laboratory technology, or any combination); and Training — either completion of an approved/accredited clinical laboratory or medical laboratory training program, which may be included in the 60 semester hours specified above or at least three months of documented laboratory training in each specialty in which the individual performs high complexity testing;

7. ON OR BEFORE 2/28/92 qualified or could have qualified as a technologist under 42 CFR 493.1433 laboratory regulations published March 14, 1990 (55 FR 9538);

8. On or before April 24, 1995, with a high school degree or equivalent and either have graduated from an approved or accredited medical laboratory or clinical laboratory training program or have successfully completed at least a 50 week official U.S. military medical laboratory procedures course and have held the military enlisted occupational specialty of Medical Laboratory Specialist (Laboratory Technician).

- *D6171 — §493.1489(b)(2): "An associate degree in a laboratory science" is interpreted to mean an associate degree in a chemical or biological science.*

Issues and Answers

How should you use the CLIA rules and Interpretive Guidelines if inspected by CMS?

- For moderate and high complexity testing, the laboratory needs to identify the individuals(s) filling each position and how each qualifies, including academic degree completed, special training, board certification, licensure (if needed), initial orientation to testing and how competency is maintained.
- Make sure that individuals actually do qualify for the designated position through education and experience.
- Try to qualify as many individuals for each position so that the responsibilities for the positions are always met.
- The titles identified by CMS do not have to correspond to working titles used within the laboratory and the specific qualifications for each title vary according to the complexity of testing.
- Keep permanent records of the information. CMS does not specify where the records should be maintained, but they must be available to the inspector.
- Be inspection-ready by being very familiar with the *Interpretive Guidelines and Probes* identified in Appendix C of the State Operations Manual.

How should you use the CLIA rules and Interpretive Guidelines if inspected by a professional accrediting organization?

- JCAHO and COLA adhere to the same personnel standards for moderate and high complexity testing as CLIA so the CLIA requirements must be followed as described.
- JCAHO, however, does have personnel standards for waived testing (WT).
    - WT.1.20—identification of staff responsible for performing and supervising the testing activities;

- WT.1.30 — documentation that testing personnel have adequate, specific training and orientation to perform the tests, and demonstrate satisfactory levels of competence (JCAHO emphasizes the importance of adequate skill level of all testing personnel including those just performing waived tests. The initial training and ongoing competency assessment ([at least every 12 months after the first year of testing] must be documented); and,
- WT.1.40 — proof that all testing personnel have access to approved, current written policies and procedures governing specific testing-related processes are current and readily available.

- CAP's personnel standards generally follow for all test complexity levels those identified by CLIA for high complexity testing.
  - CAP prefers that the laboratory director, regardless of test complexity level, be a physician or Ph.D. trained scientist.

    § (GEN.50000) Is the laboratory director a physician or a doctoral level clinical scientist qualified by training, expertise and experience in the areas of testing offered by the laboratory?

- CAP does allow the qualifications of testing personnel to vary depending on the complexity of testing performed.

    § (GEN.54750) For laboratories subject to US federal regulations, do all testing personnel meet CLIA88 requirements?

    – There must be evidence in personnel records that all testing personnel have been evaluated against CLIA88 requirements, and that all individuals qualify.

DOs and DON'Ts

- DON'T confuse the new single "non-waived" category with its **one** set of quality requirements for analytical testing and the continuing **two** categories of personnel for "moderate complexity testing" and "high complexity testing." **There still are two sets of personnel standards.**
- DO review the complexity classifications for your methods and instruments and sort out those in the moderate and high complexity categories.
- DO review the personnel requirements that are applicable for moderate and/or high complexity testing.
- DO identify the organization that will inspect and accredit your laboratory to further identify the qualifications required for the laboratory personnel.

References

1. CLIA Final Rule (codification of all previous rules (1992-January 24, 2003). http://www.phppo.cdc.gov/clia/regs/toc.aspx

2. Appendix C of SOM, Regulations and Interpretive Guidelines for Laboratories and Laboratory Services, http://www.cms.gov/clia/appendc.asp

3. Listing of government-approved certification boards for clinical consultants and directors of high complexity testing: http://www.cms.gov/clia/dirclcon.asp

4. CAP Laboratory Accreditation Checklists. College of American Pathologists (CAP). 325 Waukegan Road, Northfield, IL 60093-2750 http://www.cap.org/apps/docs/laboratory_accreditation/checklists/checklistftp.html

5. Accreditation Manual for Pathology and Clinical laboratory Services. Joint Commission on Accreditation of Healthcare Organizations (JCAHO). Oakbrook Terrace, IL. 60181

6. COLA Accreditation Manual. 9881 Broken Land Parkway, Suite 200, Columbia, MD 21046.

5: Quality Assessment of Non-Analytic Systems

One of the highly publicized changes in the CLIA Final Rule [1] was the reorganization of the quality related standards to follow the path of a specimen through pre-analytic, analytic, and post-analytic parts of the total testing process. The Final Rule specifically identifies quality requirements for the general laboratory system and the pre-analytical, analytic, and post-analytical parts. Most of the Final Rule still focuses on the analytic requirements, as does this book, but this chapter considers requirements for non-analytic quality assessment, i.e., general laboratory, pre-analytic, and post-analytic quality systems.

Final Rules: General Laboratory Systems

§ 493.1230 General laboratory systems. Each laboratory that performs nonwaived testing must meet the applicable general laboratory systems requirements in 493.1231 through 493.1236, unless HHS approves a procedure, specified in Appendix C of the State Operations Manual (CMS Pub. 7) that provides equivalent quality testing. The laboratory must monitor and evaluate the overall quality of the general laboratory systems and correct identified problems as specified in 493.1239 for each specialty and subspecialty of testing performed.

- The requirements in 493.1231 through 493.1236 deal with the
    - ❍ confidentiality of patient information,
    - ❍ specimen identification and integrity,
    - ❍ complaint investigation of problems reported to the laboratory,
    - ❍ communication breakdowns between the laboratory and its users,
    - ❍ personnel competency assessment policies for laboratory employees, and
    - ❍ evaluation of proficiency testing performance.

§ 493.1239 General laboratory systems assessment. (a) The laboratory must establish and follow written policies and procedures for an ongoing mechanism to monitor, assess, and, when indicated, correct problems identified in the general laboratory system requirements at 493.1231 through 493.1236. (b) The general laboratory systems assessment must include a review of the effectiveness or corrective actions taken to resolve problems, revision of policies and procedures necessary to prevent recurrence of problems, and discussion of general laboratory systems assessment reviews with appropriate staff. (c) The laboratory must document general laboratory systems assessment activities.

- Quality assessment must cover the general laboratory procedures and processes, monitor problems in these processes, and assure improvements.
- Laboratories will need to pay attention to the areas of confidentiality of patient information, complaint investigation, and communication breakdowns because policies and procedures in these areas have less history and likely need more care and attention.
- Laboratories generally have well-established policies and procedures for specimen identification and integrity, but often have difficulties applying their policies when physicians insist that analyses be performed even when there are issues about proper identification (e.g., proper labeling of specimen container) and specimen integrity (e.g., a hemolysed specimen). CLIA strengthens the laboratory's role here, but saying no to the doctor may result in a complaint that may also need to be investigated as part of the quality assessment of general laboratory systems.
- Personnel competency assessment, while not a new requirement, is still problematic, particularly in Point-of-Care testing sites.
- Proficiency testing requirements were perhaps the main focus in the implementation of the original rules in 1992, therefore PT policies and procedures are well established. Laboratories

still need to pay attention to those tests that are NOT presently included in PT and peer-comparison programs because they also require periodic validation of accuracy – twice a year.

Issues and Answers

What's the best source of information for guidance about general laboratory systems?

The CAP Laboratory General Checklist provides much more detail about general laboratory systems and the critical factors that might be checked during an inspection [2]. They include standards for the collection manual, phlebotomy, transport services, requisitions and specimen receipt/assessment, reporting of results, as well as laboratory computer services.

What approaches are considered acceptable for assessing the competency of personnel?

CMS leaves this up to the laboratory and provides no guidance in the Interpretive Guidelines. However, the SOM [3] provides extensive descriptions of the responsibilities and qualifications for all levels of personnel. See section 6, Subpart M, Personnel, which is 61 pages long.

The CAP Laboratory General Checklist is more helpful and lists the following elements that could be part of competency assessment in GEN.55500:

1. direct observations of routine patient test performance, including patient preparation, if applicable, specimen handling, processing and testing;
2. monitoring the recording and reporting of test results;
3. review of intermediate test results or worksheets, quality control records, proficiency testing results, and preventive maintenance records;
4. direct observation of performance of instrument maintenance and function checks;
5. assessment of test performance through testing previously analyzed specimens, internal blind testing samples or external proficiency testing samples; and

6. evaluation of problem-solving skills.

Competency assessment turns out to be a very qualitative evaluation often based on review and observation. We personally feel there should be a bigger role for using internal QC, proficiency testing, and comparison of test results between methods to demonstrate competency on a continuous basis, rather than depend on semi-annual or annual reviews. In particular, the requirement for periodic comparison of test results between analytic systems [493.1281] can be implemented to provide daily or weekly comparisons, rotating the responsibility amongst all the testing personnel, and providing an ongoing mechanism for competency assessment that assures personnel will get the correct results on real patient specimens.

Are more tests now included in proficiency testing surveys?

More tests will probably be scored because of changes in the grading criterion, but the list of tests remains the same. See Appendix 1 for the CLIA PT list of tests and criteria for acceptable performance. The grading requirement for an individual PT sample has been changed from 90% to 80% consensus, which should increase the number of tests that are actually graded. For tests not graded, given unsatisfactory grades, or not covered by approved proficiency testing programs, the laboratory is required to verify their accuracy, after each proficiency testing event (for those included in the CLIA PT list) or twice per year (for those not included in the CLIA PT list).

- Remember that a laboratory needs to achieve 4 correct results out of the 5 specimens in a PT testing event, which means the lowest acceptable score is 80%. You can see the problem caused by a single specimen that cannot be graded due to the lack of consensus agreement among laboratories. In the past, a non-graded specimen essentially counted as a correct result in the score for that event.

- **D5215** of Appendix C of the State Operations Manual specifically advises inspectors to pay attention to PT results that are not graded and result in an artificial score of 100% on a survey. It also points out the need for the laboratory to document performance in cases where the laboratory did not test a particular PT specimen.

- ❍ <u>Probes 493.1236(b)(2).</u> *Has the laboratory reviewed its test menu to determine if it tests any analyte(s) that are not listed in subpart I? [Refer to the CLIA PT list in Appendix 1.]*

- ❍ <u>Probes 493.1236(c)(2).</u> *How does a laboratory verify accuracy of tests not included under subpart I or tests for which compatible PT samples are not available (e.g., blind testing or materials with known values, other external assessment programs, split samples with another laboratory instrument or method, comparison with Kodachrome slides from a reference source)?*

Final Rules: Preanalytic Systems

§ 493.1240 Preanalytic systems. Each laboratory that performs nonwaived testing must meet the applicable preanalytic system(s) requirements in 493.1241[test requests] and 493.1241 [specimen submission, handling, referral], unless HHS approves a procedure, specified in Appendix C of the State Operations Manual that provides equivalent quality testing.

- For test requests, the laboratory should have a written or electronic request for patient testing from an authorized person, but is also allowed to accept oral requests if it solicits a written or electronic authorization within 30 days.

  - ❍ The test request must document the authorizing person by name, address or suitable identifier, as well as the individual responsible for using the test results, or the name and address of the laboratory submitting the specimen, in which case a contact person must also be identified to facilitate reporting of panic or alert values. The test request should also include the patient name or unique patient identifier, sex and age or date of birth, tests to be performed, source of the specimen, date and time of specimen collection, and any other information relevant to ensure accurate and timely testing and reporting.

- For specimen requirements for submission, handling, and referral, the laboratory must follow written policies and procedures for patient preparation, specimen collection, specimen labeling, specimen storage, specimen transport, specimen processing, specimen acceptability and rejection, and specimen referral.
    - The laboratory can only refer specimens to a laboratory that is CLIA certified or accredited by a deemed provider.
    - For referred specimens, the laboratory must provide clients with information about patient preparation, specimen collection, processing, etc.

§ 493.1249 Preanalytic systems assessment. (a) The laboratory must establish and follow written policies and procedures for an ongoing mechanism to monitor, assess, and when indicated, correct problems identified in the preanalytic systems. (b) The preanalytic assessment must include a review of the effectiveness of corrective actions taken to resolve problems, revision of policies and procedures necessary to prevent recurrence of problems, and discussion of preanalytic systems assessment review with appropriate staff. (c) The laboratory must document all preanalytic systems assessment activities.

- This is the standard language for quality assessment that is now found throughout the CLIA regulations.
- The laboratory needs to have a mechanism for monitoring the effectiveness of the patient test request policies and patient specimen processing procedures.
- The laboratory has similar responsibilities for tests that are sent out to other referral laboratories.

Issues and Answers

Isn't the allowance for an oral test request inherently contradictory to the requirements for a written test request?

That makes for an interesting conflict, doesn't it? How does the laboratory collect all the needed information if the request is made by telephone? Just soliciting a written or electronic confirmation of the oral test request isn't very satisfactory if it will take up to 30 days to get the information. And this will certainly contribute to problems with communications, which is part of what should be eliminated by having good general and pre-analytic systems. In short, this contradiction reflects the poor state of data management in healthcare today, the lack of effective computer systems, the lack of electronic patient records, and sometimes the lack of support for electronic test requisitions.

- *D5303 Interpretive Guidelines. Review the laboratory's policy for requesting written orders within 30 days of the oral requests. If no written order was received, verify the laboratory has documentation showing the attempt.* Since when was quality about trying to do the right thing right? Good intentions seem to be enough for CLIA in this case, even though that might not be good enough for our patients!
- CAP GEN.40935 requires that the laboratory have a policy that personnel receiving verbal or phone orders must read back the entire order to verify accuracy of transcription.

It's one thing to have a policy for specimen acceptability, but how do you enforce it when physicians ask for exceptions?

The application of the policy at the bench level must be uniform and ideally there should be no exceptions. More realistically, there is a need for a mechanism to review a specific request for an exception, e.g., there may be compelling grounds where no information is worse than information of limited quality interpreted with caution. The laboratory's Medical Director must be involved in developing the policy and providing guidelines for implementation. Any decision to override the policy requires the careful judgment of an experienced professional, who has been delegated such authority. The decision would need to take into account the test requested and the specific effect of the conditions on that test. If the Medical Director is not actively involved in the development and support of the policy, proper implementation and enforcement will be difficult.

Is a laboratory subject to the requirements for referral services if physicians are accessing those services directly?

CAP makes it clear that the Laboratory Director must be involved in the selection of any referral laboratories (GEN.41370) and has a responsibility for monitoring the quality of test results received from reference laboratories (GEN.41350). The other responsibilities for quality assessment of preanalytic (as well as postanalytic) systems for referred testing likewise apply, according to CAP.

Final Rules: Postanalytic Systems

§ 493.1290 Postanalytic systems Each laboratory... same old, same old, blah, blah, blah – it's all about reporting the results of laboratory tests!

§ 493.1291 Test report. *(a) The laboratory must have adequate manual or electronic systems in place to ensure test results and other patient-specific data are accurately and reliably sent from the point of data entry to final report destination in a timely manner. (b) Test report information maintained as part of the patient's chart or medical record must be readily available to the laboratory and to CMS or a CMS agent upon request. (c) The test reports must indicate the following:*

- *Patient's name and identification number, or an unique patient identifier and identification number;*
- *Name and address of the laboratory location where test was performed;*
- *Test report date;*
- *Test performed;*
- *Specimen source, when appropriate;*
- *Test result and, if applicable, units of measurement or interpretation, or both;*
- *Any information regarding the condition and disposition of specimens that do not meet the laboratory's criteria for acceptability.*

(d) Pertinent "reference intervals" or "normal" values must be available to the authorized person who ordered the test. (e) Laboratory must, upon request, make available to clients a list of test methods employed by the laboratory and, as applicable, the performance specifications established or verified in 493.1253. (f) Test results must be released only to authorized persons. (g) The laboratory must immediately alert the individual or entity requesting the test... when any test result indicates an imminent life-threatening condition, or panic or alert values. (h) When the laboratory cannot report patient test results within its established time frames, the laboratory must determine, based on the urgency of the patient test(s) requested, the need to notify the appropriate individual(s) of the delayed testing. (i) If a laboratory refers patient specimens for testing

- *The referring laboratory must not revise results or information directly related to the interpretation of results provided by the testing laboratory;*
- *The referring laboratory may permit each testing laboratory to send the test result directly to the authorized person who initially requested the test. The referring laboratory must retain or be able to produce an exact duplicate of each testing laboratory's report; and*
- *The authorized person who orders a test must be notified by the referring laboratory of the name and address of each laboratory location where the test was performed.*

(j) All test reports or records of the information on the test reports must be maintained by the laboratory in a manner that permits ready identification and timely accessibility. (k) When errors in the reported patient test results are detected, the laboratory must do the following:

- *Promptly notify the authorized person ordering the test...*
- *Issue corrected reports promptly...*
- *Maintain duplicates of the original report, as well as the corrected report.*

§ 493.1299 Postanalytic systems assessment. (a) The laboratory must establish and follow written policies and procedures for an ongoing mechanism to monitor, assess and, when indicated, correct problems identified in the postanalytic systems....(b) The

postanalytic systems assessment must include a review of the effectiveness of corrective actions taken to resolve problems, revision of policies and procedures necessary to prevent recurrence of problems, and discussion of postanalytic systems assessment reviews with appropriate staff. (c) The laboratory must document all postanalytic systems assessment activities.

- This is the standard language for quality assessment that is now found throughout the CLIA regulations.
- The laboratory needs to have a mechanism for monitoring the effectiveness of the test reporting procedures and processes, as well as the contents of the test report.
- The laboratory has similar responsibilities for tests that are sent out to other referral laboratories.

Issues and Answers

Are there any guidelines for panic values?

Not in the CLIA rules or SOM materials. However, you can generally find published guidelines in textbooks, journals, and the Internet. An Internet search for "panic values" will get you started. Ultimately, the laboratory's Medical Director must be involved in setting the values, approving the list of tests, and establishing the policy for communicating panic values.

If a test report is corrected, is it necessary to maintain the earlier erroneous report?

Yes, the laboratory is required to have copies of both in the records. It is very important to be able to distinguish the correct from the incorrect results.

- *D5821 Interpretive Guidelines: The laboratory must have a system for maintaining copies of the original and corrected reports.*
- *D5821 Probes: For laboratories that maintain the patient's medical record as the test reports, what is the mechanism for differentiating between the incorrect original report and the corrected report?*

DO's and DON'Ts

- DO pay special attention to the CAP and JCAHO guidelines that apply to general quality systems, as well as pre-analytical and post-analytical systems. They often provide more detailed information on what inspectors will ask. In particular, CAP provides good information about quality system requirements for the Laboratory Information System.

- DO expect that inspectors will pay special attention to pre-analytic and post-analytic requirements. The analytic requirements have been around from the beginning and it is often thought (or, more correctly, hoped) that problems in this area have been taken care of by now.

- DO pay particular attention to JCAHO's new "tracer" methodology, by which an inspector will track specific patients and their specimens through the entire laboratory testing process. That methodology provides a very efficient way to review the effectiveness of all laboratory systems, analytic as well as non-analytic.

- DON'T forget to carefully document your investigation of customer complaints. Customers are much more likely to complain about non-analytic systems because those problems are easier for them to recognize than problems with analytical quality. Customers can be expected to complain about the timeliness of services, plus what they may consider to be "hassles" in specimen acquisition, processing, and acceptance.

- DO make sure your non-analytic policies and procedures are in order so that they can be referenced in any investigation of customer complaints and documentation of corrective actions.

- DON'T panic over non-analytic systems. You've actually been doing this forever and you just need to be sure you've got everything written down and everyone following the written policies and procedures.

References

1. CLIA Final Rule (codification of all previous rules (1992-January 24, 2003). http://www.phppo.cdc.gov/clia/regs/toc.aspx

2. CAP Laboratory Accreditation Checklists. College of American Pathologists (CAP). 325 Waukegan Road, Northfield, IL 60093-2750 http://www.cap.org/apps/docs/laboratory_accreditation/checklists/checklistftp.html

3. Appendix C of SOM, Regulations and Interpretive Guidelines for Laboratories and Laboratory Services, http://www.cms.gov/clia/appendc.asp

4. Accreditation Manual for Pathology and Clinical laboratory Services. Joint Commission on Accreditation of Healthcare Organizations (JCAHO). Oakbrook Terrace, IL. 60181

6: Final Method Validation Requirements

Until the Final CLIA Rule was published, many laboratories escaped the requirements to validate the performance of their methods. The February 28, 1992 rules [1] provided an exception for laboratories that performed moderately complex tests using unmodified FDA-approved analytical methods and systems. These sites could accept the manufacturer's performance specifications in lieu of performing method validation studies themselves. All this changed on January 24, 2003 with the issuance of Final CLIA Rule [2]. ALL non-waived (moderate and high complexity) testing methods now require in-lab validation of method performance.

While CLIA sets the minimum testing requirements, testing sites can and do choose to meet the requirements of other accreditation organizations with CLIA-deemed status (which may have more stringent requirements), such as the Joint Commission for Accreditation of Healthcare Organizations (JCAHO) [3], the College of American Pathologists (CAP) [4], and the Commission on Office Laboratory Accreditation (COLA)[5]. There are also state health laboratory organizations in Washington and New York, which are approved by the government (have exempt status) and impose specific requirements. In addition, it is always important to keep in mind those practices that would be expected as part of professional responsibility and good laboratory practice.

General requirements for quality assessment of laboratory tests

CLIA provides a broad framework for quality systems that are organized around the flow of a specimen through the laboratory. Subpart K, Quality Systems for Nonwaived Testing, begins with the general requirements:

§493.1200 (a) Each laboratory that performs nonwaived testing must establish and maintain written policies and procedures that implement and monitor quality systems for all phases of the total

testing process (that is, preanalytic, analytic, and postanalytic), as well as general laboratory systems. (b) The laboratory's quality systems must include a quality assessment component that ensures continuous improvement of the laboratory's performance and services through ongoing monitoring that identifies, evaluates and resolves problems. (c) The various components of the laboratory's quality system are used to meet the requirements in this part and must be appropriate for the specialties and subspecialties of testing the laboratory performs, services it offers, and clients it serves.

§493.1250, Analytic Systems, requires laboratories to meet the requirements for the following:

- **§493.1251 Procedure manual**
- **§493.1252 Test systems, equipment, instruments, reagents, materials, and supplies**
- **§493.1253 Establishment and verification of method performance specifications**
- **§493.1254 Maintenance and function checks**
- **§493.1255 Calibration and calibration verification procedures**
- **§493.1256 Control procedures**
- **§493.1261-1278 Specialty and subspecialty requirements**
- **§493.1281 Comparison of test results**
- **§493.1282 Corrective actions**
- **§493.1283 Test records**
- **§493.1289 Analytic systems assessment**

In this chapter, we consider the requirements for the "establishment and verification of method performance specifications," i.e., method validation.

Method Validation and Test Complexity

The recommendations that must be followed depend on the "complexity" of the test. The CLIA Final Rule combines moderate and high complexity into a Non-Waived classification that governs method validation. Information about classification of specific test methods is available from the CMS website at the address: http://www.cms.gov/clia/

Waived Tests. The minimum requirement for waived testing under CLIA is to follow the manufacturer's directions. There are no requirements for method validation.

Non-Waived Tests Approved by FDA. Most tests performed in laboratories today fall in this category, thus most method validation studies should follow the recommendations in section §493.1253:

§493.1253 Establishment and verification of performance specifications.

(a) Applicability. Laboratories are not required to verify or establish performance specifications for any test system used by the laboratory before April 24, 2003.

(b)(1) Verification of performance specifications. Each laboratory that introduces an unmodified, FDA-cleared or approved test system must do the following before reporting patient test results:

(i) Demonstrate that it can obtain performance specifications comparable to those established by the manufacturer for the following performance characteristics:

(A) Accuracy.

(B) Precision.

(C) Reportable range of test results for the test system.

(ii) Verify that the manufacturer's reference intervals (normal values) are appropriate for the laboratory's patient population.

This would generally mean performing four experiments:

- comparison of methods experiment to estimate inaccuracy/ bias,
- replication experiment to estimate imprecision,

- linearity-type experiment to determine the reportable range, and
- Collecting reference values to verify the reference range [alternatively, the laboratory medical director can document that the manufacturer's ranges or textbook ranges are appropriate for the clientele being served].

Non-Waived Tests Modified or Developed In-House. Testing sites that modify moderate complexity tests or use tests developed in-house or tests classified as high complexity under CLIA must follow more stringent method validation requirements, as follows:

§493.1253 (b)(2) Each laboratory that modifies an FDA-cleared or approved test system, or introduces a test system not subject to FDA clearance or approval (including methods developed in-house and standardized methods such as text book procedures, Gram stain, or potassium hydroxide preparations), or uses a test system in which performance specifications are not provided by the manufacturer must, before reporting patient test results, establish for each test system the performance specifications for the following performance characteristics, as applicable:

(i) Accuracy.
(ii) Precision.
(iii) Analytical sensitivity.
(iv) Analytical specificity to include interfering substances.
(v) Reportable range of test results for the test system.
(vi) Reference intervals (normal values).
(vii) Any other performance characteristic required for test performance.

This would mean performing seven different experiments:

- comparison of methods experiment to estimate inaccuracy/bias
- replication experiment to estimate imprecision,
- detection limit experiment for estimating constant interferences,
- interference and recovery experiments for assessing specificity and potential interfering substances,
- linearity experiment to determine the reportable range, and
- more extensive reference value study to estimate the reference range(s).

Plus, there are additional requirements that the laboratory establish calibration and control procedures that take into account the performance observed for a method.

§493.1253 (3) Determination of calibration and control procedures. The laboratory must determine the test system's calibration procedures and control procedures based upon the performance specifications verified or established under paragraphs (b)(1) or (b)(2) of this section.

The requirements for calibration and control procedures are described in more detail in sections 493.1255 Standard for calibration and calibration verification procedures and 493.1256 Standard for control procedures. We will discuss the calibration issues in more detail in Chapter 8 and the control issues in Chapters 11 through 14.

Finally, section §493.1253(c) requires that the laboratory must have documentation of the verification or establishment of all applicable test performance specifications. Method validation data should be kept in a permanent file and kept for at least as long as the method is in use.

It is important to note that these requirements are NOT retroactive, meaning that any method in use prior to the implementation of the new CLIA Final Rules on April 24, 2003 need not be re-verified under CLIA.

Additional requirements for periodic validation of method performance. There are two other requirements that may lead to additional method validation studies for certain tests.

- Ongoing (at least semi-annual) assessment of accuracy is required for any tests that are not evaluated by a proficiency testing program.

  §493.1236 Evaluation of proficiency testing performance. (c) At least twice annually, the laboratory must verify the accuracy of the following: (1) Any test or procedure it performs that is not included in subpart I of this part. (2) Any test or procedure listed in subpart I of this part for which compatible proficiency testing samples are not offered by a CMS-approved proficiency testing program.

- Tests that are performed by multiple analytical systems require periodic comparison, as described below:

§493.1281 Comparison of test results. (a) If a laboratory performs the same test using different methodologies or instruments, or performs the same test at multiple testing sites, the laboratory must have a system that twice a year evaluates and defines the relationship between test results using different methodologies, instruments, or testing sites.

JCAHO standards for method validation [3]

Waived tests. JCAHO recognizes waived test methodologies as defined by CLIA'88, but unlike CLIA requires more than just following manufacturer's directions. JCAHO's waived testing standard WT.1.4, "policies and procedures governing specific testing-related processes are current and readily available," includes equipment performance evaluation. For laboratories to meet this standard, JCAHO wants evidence (available for surveyors' review) that all tests are meeting the needs of the testing site's clientele. The evidence includes: accuracy, precision, and reportable range (validity of low and high values) data. In addition, someone (i.e., the testing site's director) will need to verify that the reference ranges taken from the manufacturer's product inserts or elsewhere are appropriate.

For JCAHO, it is only necessary to evaluate the method, not all instruments, e.g., all glucose meters, once. As part of JCAHO's total quality management philosophy, performance history, including QC data, can be used as the "evidence" of adequate method performance when a method used in one location is instituted in another.

Non-Waived (Moderate and High Complexity) Tests Approved by FDA. While JCAHO requires the same general QC requirements as CLIA, JCAHO also has specific method validation requirements (QC.1.7). JCAHO identifies the elements of QC.1.7 as follows:

- Before a new test method is used to report patient results, the laboratory verifies that the method will produce accurate results consistently and reliably;

- The laboratory has a documented validation for each new method implemented in the two years before survey;
- The laboratory at least verifies accuracy, precision, and reportable range for a patient-testing procedure that is an approved, unmodified test of moderate complexity for which the manufacturer has established the performance specifications;
- The laboratory verifies the manufacturer's performance specifications that include accuracy, precision, analytical sensitivity, analytical specificity, the reportable range, and the reference ranges(s) for modified tests of moderate complexity or high complexity tests including the following
    - Test procedures with modifications to the FDA-approved use for specimen type, reagents, instrument, procedural steps, or other components;
    - Tests or methods classified by the FDA as high complexity;
    - Tests or methods developed in the laboratory with no FDA evaluation;
- For each new test method, the laboratory has made the determination that the reference range applies to the specific patient population(s) tested.

As with waived test methods, JCAHO accepts QC data and test performance history as the "evidence" of adequate method performance when a method used in one location is instituted in another location.

CAP's Laboratory Accreditation Program standards for method validation [4]

CAP's philosophy is that all clinical laboratory testing, including even CLIA waived tests, needs to meet the requirements defined under Section §493.1253(b)(2) of CLIA '88.

The 2003 CAP Checklist GEN (Laboratory General) includes performance specification requirements – accuracy and precision (GEN: 42020), reportable range (GEN: 42161), sensitivity or the lower detection limit (GEN: 42025), and reference range (GEN:

42163) – for each test procedure. Specificity (GEN: 42030) implies an evaluation of the method's ability to respond correctly to the concentration of analyte in the presence of interfering substances. CAP's Checklist now states: "The laboratory must verify or establish method performance specifications for analytic interferences. Interfering substances pose a significant problem to the clinical laboratory and healthcare providers who may be misled by laboratory results that do not reflect patient clinical status. The laboratory must be aware of common interferences by performing studies or having available studies performed elsewhere (such as by the instrument/reagent manufacturer)."

Issues and Answers

What is the consequence (in terms of method validation studies) of modifying a manufacturer's method?

- Section §493.1253(b)(2) of the CLIA requirements states that when a laboratory modifies an FDA-cleared or approved test system **(meaning a method classified as waived or moderate complexity)** it must, before reporting patient test results, establish the performance specifications for — accuracy, precision, analytical sensitivity, analytical specificity to include interfering substances, reportable range of test results, reference intervals (normal values), and any other performance characteristic required for test performance.
    - For a lab inspected by CMS for CLIA compliance, this means that whenever a waived test method is modified, all the above performance specifications would need to be evaluated. Under CLIA, no evaluation of these parameters is required for waived testing.
    - For a moderately complex test under section §493.1253(b)(1), the lab is required to evaluate all of the above specifications except analytical sensitivity and specificity and any other performance characteristics required for test performance. By modifying the FDA-approved system these additional characteristics would need to be evaluated.

- These six specifications plus any other performance characteristic needed also must be evaluated for all methods classified as high complexity as well as methods developed in-house.

What are the CLIA surveyors looking for in terms of method verification?

- In addition to the experiments previously identified, the CMS State Operations Manual Appendix C, Regulations and Interpretive Guidelines for Laboratories and Laboratory Services, under the D-tag numbers of **D5421 – D5425** provide helpful information in its *Interpretive Guidelines and Probes* sections. Below are examples from these two sections under **D5421 (§493.1253(b)(1)):**
  - *When a temporary replacement (loaner) instrument is received which is identical (i.e., same make and model, and method for the same analyte) to the instrument which is being replaced, the laboratory must verify comparable performance by comparing, at a minimum, results of two or more levels of controls and either previously tested proficiency samples or previously tested patient specimens.*
  - *If a method was verified by someone other than the laboratory staff (e.g., manufacturer representative), the laboratory must demonstrate that this verification correlates with its in-house test performance. This may be accomplished by the laboratory testing "known" samples.*
    - § *Probes §493.1253(b)(1) How does the laboratory determine if a new or revised LIS program (whether purchased or developed in-house) performs acceptably before it is integrated into routine operation?*

DOs and DON'Ts

- DO identify the organization that will inspect and accredit your laboratory to determine the approach to method validation.
- DO review the complexity classifications for your methods and instruments to determine whether and what method validation is needed.

- DO remember that JCAHO and CAP, unlike CLIA, require method validation for waived as well as non-waived test methodologies.
- DON'T modify any methods unless you're prepared to expend considerably more time and effort in validating method performance.
- DON'T omit method validation for waived test methods just because you are inspected for CLIA compliance. Good laboratory practice dictates knowing whether *any* method meets the needs of your testing site's clientele.

References

1. U.S. Department of Health and Human Services. Medicare, Medicaid and CLIA programs: Regulations implementing the Clinical Laboratory Improvement Amendments of 1988 (CLIA). Final rule. *Fed Regist* 1992; 57:7002-186.

2. US Centers for Medicare & Medicaid Services (CMS). Medicare, Medicaid, and CLIA Programs: Laboratory Requirements Relating to quality Systems and Certain Personnel Qualifications. Final Rule. Fed Regist Jan 24 2003;16:3640-3714.

3. CLIA Final Rule (codification of all previous rules (1992-Jan. 24. 2003). http://www.phppo.cdc.gov/clia/regs/toc.aspx

4. CMS State Operations Manual Appendix C, Regulations and Interpretive Guidelines for Laboratories and Laboratory Services, http://www.cms.gov/clia/appendc.asp

5. CMS Website for CLIA'88: www.cms.hhs.gov/clia/

6. CAP Laboratory Accreditation Checklists. College of American Pathologists (CAP). 325 Waukegan Road, Northfield, IL 60093-2750 http://www.cap.org/apps/docs/laboratory_accreditation/checklists/checklistftp.html

7. Accreditation Manual for Pathology and Clinical laboratory Services. Joint Commission on Accreditation of Healthcare Organizations (JCAHO). Oakbrook Terrace, IL. 60181

8. COLA Accreditation Manual. 9881 Broken Land Parkway, Suite 200, Columbia, MD 21046.

9. MV – The regulations: http://www.westgard.com/guest11.htm

7: Method Validation Plan and Procedures

One of the most important changes in the CLIA Final Rule is that laboratories must now perform method validation studies for all non-waived methods implemented after April 24, 2003. Remember that moderate complexity methods are now treated the same as high complexity methods and are combined under the new term "non-waived methods." Test systems in use prior to April 24, 2003 do *NOT* require validation.

The CLIA Rules

The requirements for method validation are given as follows [1]:

§493.1253 (b)(1) Verification of performance specifications. Each laboratory that introduces an unmodified, FDA-cleared or approved test system must do the following before reporting patient test results:

(i) Demonstrate that it can obtain performance specifications comparable to those established by the manufacturer for the following performance characteristics:

a. Accuracy

b. Precision

c. Reportable range of test results for the test system

(ii) Verify that the manufacturer's reference intervals (normal values) are appropriate for the laboratory's patient population.

For non-FDA cleared methods, or methods modified by the laboratory, the list of performance characteristics is expanded to include:

- **analytical sensitivity (or detection limit),**
- **analytical specificity (or interfering substances),**
- **reference intervals, and**
- **any other performance characteristic required for the particular test and system.**

Definitions of terms

The following terms are defined in the Final Rule [1, page 3702]:

- ***Test system.*** The instructions and all of the instrumentation, equipment, reagents, and supplies needed to perform an assay or examination and generate test results.
- ***FDA-cleared or approved test system.*** A test system cleared or approved by the FDA through the premarket notification (510k) or premarket approval (PMA) process for in-vitro diagnostic use.
- ***Reportable range.*** The span of test result values over which the laboratory can establish or verify the accuracy of the instrument or test system measurement response.

The State Operations Manual [2] clarifies the meaning of a modified method by listing examples of changes that are considered modifications of the manufacturer's FDA-cleared or approved test system.

- ***Modified method.*** **D5423** describes "modified by the laboratory" as meaning anything that might affect the performance specifications, including all of the following:

  - *Using a different sample matrix (plasma vs. urine);*
  - *Using or promoting the test for another purpose (screening vs. diagnostic);*
  - *Changing the type of analysis (qualitative results reported as quantitative);*
  - *Change in specimen handling instructions;*
  - *Incubation times or temperatures;*
  - *Change in specimen or reagent dilution;*
  - *Using a different calibration material (or changing the manufacturer's set-points);*
  - *Changing or elimination of a procedural step;*
  - *Change or addition of detector (conjugate) or substrate;*
  - *Change in solid phase;*
  - *Change in the cutoff or method of calculating the cutoff for semi-quantitative assays;*

- *Change in the endpoint or calculation of the endpoint;*
- *Addition of adsorbent;*
- *Change in the strain of antigen in serologic assays; and*
- *Changing the calibrator/reference material.*

An important point – don't play around with a manufacturer's method and the recommendations for use! If you make any changes, you become liable for proving that those changes do not affect the performance characteristics of the method. That will require extensive validation studies.

The definitions of other important terms can be found in the *Basic Method Validation* manual [3], which references sources such as NCCLS [4]:

- ***Accuracy.*** Closeness of the agreement between the result of a measurement and the true value of the measurand. Usually expressed in the same units as the result, as the difference between the true value and the observed value, or as a percentage of the true value that the difference represents; expressed this way the quantity is more correctly termed 'inaccuracy' [from NCCLS]. Note that this represents the total error concept of accuracy because the difference between the observed value and the true value could be due to random error, systematic error, or the total error from both. The more traditional concept of accuracy has been to consider just the systematic error or "bias."
- ***Precision.*** The closeness of agreement between independent test results obtained under prescribed conditions [NCCLS]. Typically described by calculating the standard deviation (s) or coefficient of variation (CV = 100*s/mean).

These terms are more readily understood by reference to the following figure. Assume that the distribution shown here represents the results for a test where many measurements have been made on an individual specimen. The "true value" for that specimen is shown by the bold vertical line. The observed mean of the measurements on the specimen is shown by the dashed vertical line. The tail end of the distribution is indicated by the dotted vertical line.

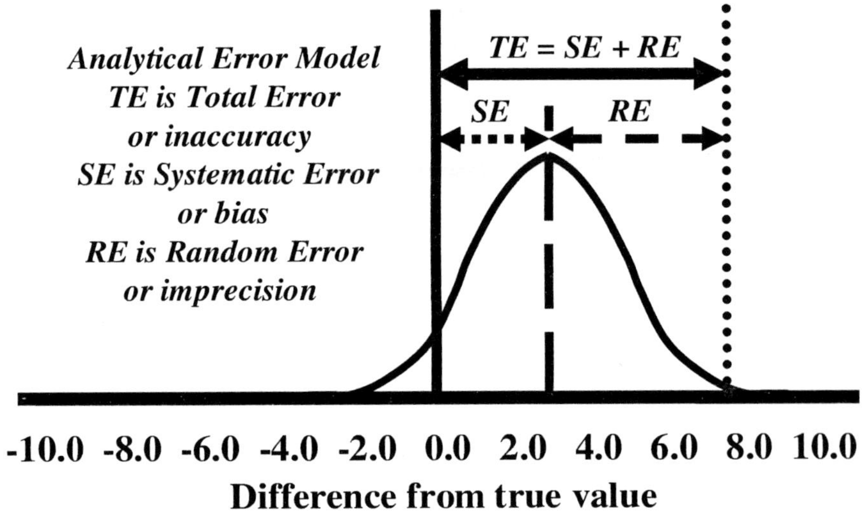

- ***Systematic error, SE***. The difference between the observed mean of the measurements and the true value is the systematic error or bias of the analytical method or test system.
- ***Random error, RE***. The width of the distribution describes the random error or imprecision of the analytical method or test system.
- ***Total error.*** The net or combined effect of random error (imprecision) and systematic error (inaccuracy) is the total error of the analytical method or test system.

For purposes of this discussion, the remaining performance characteristics can be described as follows:

- ***Reference interval.*** The expected range of values for a population of individuals in a defined state of health. Commonly called "normal range" to represent the values expect in normal healthy individuals.
- ***Detection limit.*** The smallest test value that can be distinguished from zero. Different experimental procedures

give different estimates, which are called the lower limit of detection, biological limit of detection, or functional sensitivity.

- ***Interference.*** Artifactual increase or decrease in apparent concentration or intensity of an analyte due to the presence of a substance that reacts nonspecifically with either the detection reagent or the signal itself [NCCLS].

Issues and Answers

What's the plan?

In validating the performance of a new method, it is useful to organize the experimental work as follows:

- **Familiarization period**
  - ❍ Establish a working procedure
  - ❍ Validate analyst performance (within-run replication experiment)
  - ❍ Check calibration vs other in-lab methods
- **Preliminary method validation studies**
  - ❍ Validate reportable range (linearity experiment)
  - ❍ Validate detection limit if applicable
  - ❍ Validate within-day precision (within-day replication experiment)
  - ❍ Validate interferences (interference experiment)
- **Final method validation studies**
  - ❍ Validate long-term precision (20 day replication experiment)
  - ❍ Validate accuracy (comparison of methods experiment)
  - ❍ Verify reference interval transference
- **Document performance and acceptability**
  - ❍ Prepare validation report
  - ❍ Write operating procedure

The purpose of the initial familiarization period is to be sure the method is working properly before attempting to validate its performance characteristics. The analyst's technique should be evaluated by repeating a specimen or control sample 10 to 20 times within a single run or within a few runs. It is also good to check the calibrators or standards against the other methods in the laboratory that will be used later on in the comparison of methods experiment. If systematic differences are observed, they need to be resolved before proceeding with the other validation experiments.

- **D5421** describes the verification of performance specifications, whereas **D5423** describes the establishment and verification of performance specifications. The main difference is that **D5421** discusses only precision, accuracy, and reportable range, whereas **D5423** also includes analytical sensitivity (or detection limit), analytical specificity (interfering substances), and reference intervals. Note that the plan recommended above includes all of these characteristics. The user can adapt the plan to fit the need for "verification" or "establishment" of performance specifications.
- **D5421** also specifies that *"the verification of method performance should provide evidence that the accuracy, precision, and reportable range of the procedure are adequate to meeting the clients' needs, as determined by the laboratory director and clinical consultant. A laboratory may use the manufacturer's performance specifications as guidelines, but is responsible for verifying the manufacturer's analytical claims before initiating patient testing."*

What are the experimental procedures?

Our purpose here is to provide an overview of the experimental procedures with some guidelines for minimum numbers of samples and appropriate data calculations. More detailed guidelines are provided in the *Basic Method Validation* manual and related Internet materials are available at Westgard Web (www.westgard.com).

Linearity experiment. [www.westgard.com/lesson26.htm] Once you are satisfied that the method is working properly, begin with a linearity experiment having at least 3 different solutions (better to have 5 or 6 solutions) that will span the low to high range expected for the method. Analyze these solutions in at least duplicate, preferable triplicate. Plot all the points on a graph showing the observed test values on the y-axis and the bottle value or calculated sample value on the x-axis. Draw the best straight line through the points. Inspect the plot and identify the range of values for which the observed results are consistent with the expected results. That's the reportable range over which the method provides useful results.

- **D5421** provides no specific guidance on how many different solutions to use or how to analyze the data for reportable range, but indicates that low and high calibration or control materials may be used, as well as patient specimens with known abnormal high and abnormal low values.

Replication experiment. [www.westgard.com/lesson22.htm] A minimum of 20 replicate measurements should be made on at least two levels of control materials. Depending on the time period of interest, the study can be performed within a run, within a day, or over a month. The different estimates of precision are often named to describe the time period covered, e.g., within-run or within-day. Estimates from longer terms are often called "total imprecision." Performance can be described by calculating the mean, standard deviation (s, SD), and coefficient of variation from the replication data.

- **D5421** actually specifies verification of day-to-day, run-to-run, and within-run variation, as well as operator variance. This would require an ANOVA (analysis of variance) experimental design to separate the different variance components and provide all the estimates. In practice, we think it is more practical to make an estimate of the total or day-to-day imprecision that includes operator variation. That is the worst case estimate, meaning as large as it will get, and if it is acceptable, all of the component parts are also acceptable.

- **D5421** also allows repeat testing of patient samples and calibration materials.

Detection limit experiment. [www.westgard.com/lesson29.htm] This experiment is really a replication experiment that is performed for a material of very low concentration. A "blank" material of zero concentration leads to the estimate of the lower limit of detection (LLD), which is calculated as either 2s or 3s. A material of low concentration, but not zero, is used to estimate the biological limit of detection (BLD), which is calculated as the LLD plus 2s or 3s. A material at a concentration where the method CV is 20% is used to estimate functional sensitivity (FS).

- **D5423** specifies that the *"laboratory is responsible for determining the lowest concentration or amount of the analyte or substance that can be measured or distinguished from a blank, i.e., the minimum detection limits or how much of the analyte must be present to be measured."* This suggests using LLD or BLD, but not FS.

Interference experiment. [www.westgard.com/lesson27.htm] Common interferences, such as lipemia, hemolysis, and elevated bilirubin are usually tested, along with potential interferences that are specific to the diagnostic test and the analytical methodology. The approach is to prepare "test" and "blank" solutions, add a known amount of the suspected interfering substance to the test solution, then analyze both and observe the difference between the two solutions.

- **D5423** notes that the *"laboratory must document information regarding interfering substances from product information, literature, or its own testing. These may include: specimen hemolysis, anticoagulant, lipemia, and turbidity; patients' clinical conditions, disease states, and medications."*

Comparison of methods experiment. [www.westgard.com/lesson23.htm] A minimum of 20, preferably 40 or more, patient samples are analyzed by the new method and an established method that is available to the laboratory. It is advisable to collect the comparison results over a period of at least a week in order to minimize systematic errors that might occur on a given day. Results should be plotted on a "comparison graph" with the new method's results on the y-axis and the comparison method's results on the x-axis. The appropriate data analysis is to calculate regression statistics that describe the slope, y-intercept, and standard deviation of the points around the regression line. An alternate way of analyzing the comparison data is to plot the difference of the test minus comparison result on the y-axis versus the comparison result on the x-axis. This "difference plot" should show uniform scatter above and below the zero line and throughout the concentration range. The appropriate statistical analysis for a difference plot is to calculate the t-value, the bias between methods, and the standard deviation of the difference (often called t-test analysis).

- **D5421** specifies *"testing reference materials, comparing results of tests performed by the laboratory against the results of a reference method, or comparing split sample results with results obtained from a method, which is shown to provide clinically valid results."* Any method in previous routine application would seem to satisfy the last requirement. There is no guidance on numbers of specimens, no advice on data analysis, and no probes that describe what might be considered acceptable. However, remember the upfront statement that method specifications should be *"adequate to meet the clients' needs, as determined by the laboratory director and clinical consultant."* The laboratory is responsible for doing this in an accepted and proper way.

Reference interval transference. [www.westgard.com/lesson30.htm] One advantage of calculating regression statistics for the comparison of methods data is their subsequent usefulness for assessing the appropriate reference intervals on the new analytical method or test system. The old reference limits can be used to calculate the reference limits for the new method ($Y_{new} = a + bX_{old}$, where a is the y-intercept and b the slope calculated from the comparison of methods data. A second approach is to analyze specimens from 20 normal individuals and compare their results to the manufacturer's recommended reference interval or to published recommendations. NCCLS advises that the reference interval can be used if 18 of 20 values are within the recommended interval [5]. Another option is for the Laboratory Medical Director to render a judgment on the reference intervals that are appropriate for the population being served by the laboratory (an option we call divine judgment).

- **D5423** notes that *"the laboratory may make use of the manufacturer's reference range provided it is appropriate for the laboratory's patient population (i.e., a normal range that reflects the type of specimen and demographic variables such as age and sex, as applicable). If the manufacturer has not provided reference ranges appropriate for the laboratory's patient population, the laboratory may use published reference range(s). The laboratory must evaluate an appropriate number of specimens to verify the manufacturer's claims for normal values or, as applicable, the published reference ranges."*

DO's and DON'Ts

There is surprisingly *little* guidance for method validation in Appendix C of the State Operations Manual! Therefore, it is up to you and your laboratory to have a well-defined plan and to be well-organized in carrying out the experimental procedures. Good record keeping is essential to document the conditions of the studies (reagent lot numbers, calibration lot numbers, re-calibration occurrences, scheduled preventive maintenance, and all method changes or corrective actions).

- DON'T make modifications to your methods unless you're willing and able to carry out extensive validation studies.
- DO formalize a plan for your validation studies. Take into account the characteristics that need to be tested on the basis of the method classification. If non-waived unmodified, then validate reportable range, detection limit if applicable, precision, accuracy, transference of reference intervals. If non-waived and modified, these studies should be more extensive, plus there is a need for interference testing and an extensive study to estimate reference intervals.
- DO implement your plan by preparing a set of worksheets that define the amount of data to be collected for each of the different experiments. These worksheets will help formalize the planning process and make sure the critical experimental variables are properly defined.

- ❍ The reportable range worksheet should have columns for the date, analyst, sample identification, assigned or known value, observed result #1, observed result #2, etc., average results, and comments. The number of rows will depend on the number of samples to be analyzed, a minimum of 3, but preferably 5 or 6, and possibly as many as 10. Also include information about the sources of the samples, preparation of serum pools, manufacturer and lot numbers of commercial materials, etc.

- ❍ The replication worksheet should have columns for the date, time, analyst, result for material 1, result for material 2, (result for material 3 if needed), and comments. The number of rows should be at least 20. Also include information about the manufacturer and lot numbers of the control materials. Note that a worksheet of this form can be used for within-run, within-day, or monthly replication experiments. You can also use it for the detection limit experiment.

- ❍ The comparison of methods worksheet should have columns for the date, analyst, specimen identification number, test method result (y), comparison method result (x), difference (y-x), and comments. The number of rows should be 20 to 40.

You can download free method validation worksheets at: http://www.westgard.com/mvworksheets.html

- DO plot and review the comparison data as it is accumulated. Don't wait till the end! You want to discover any discrepant values right away, while the specimens are still available for re-analysis.

- DO prepare graphs for displaying and analyzing your data. Remember that a picture is worth a thousand words. For many people, a visual display is more useful than statistical results.

- DO perform the statistical calculations that are appropriate for the data collected in the different experiments.
- DON'T calculate statistics that you don't understand. The statistics should provide a summary of the data and more exact estimates of the errors that you see in the graphical displays and assessments.

References

1. US Centers for Medicare & Medicaid Services (CMS). Medicare, Medicaid, and CLIA Programs: Laboratory Requirements Relating to quality Systems and Certain Personnel Qualifications. Final Rule. Fed Regist Jan 24 2003;16:3640-3714.

2. CMS State Operations Manual – Interpretive Guidelines: Appendix C. www.cms.gov/clia/appendc.asp

3. Westgard JO. Basic Method Validation, 2nd ed. Madison WI:Westgard QC, Inc., 2003.

4. NRSCL8-A. Terminology and definitions for use in NCCLS Documents; Approved standard. NCCLS, 940 West Valley Road, Suite 1400, Wayne, PA 19087-1898.

5. NCCLS C28-A. How to define and determine reference intervals in the clinical laboratory. NCCLS, 940 West Valley Road, Suite 1400, Wayne, PA, 19087-1898.

8: Calibration and Calibration Verification

General requirements for the validation of new methods were discussed in chapters 6 and 7. In addition, there are specific requirements for calibration and calibration verification that seem to cause a lot of confusion, which is why we are devoting a whole chapter to this topic.

Calibration is very important because it determines the relationship between the signal generated by an analytical methodology and the test results that are reported. Calibration is typically performed by analyzing two or more standard solutions, or calibrators, that have known concentrations of the material of interest. "Two-point calibration," which is very common with today's highly automated analyzers, generally involves a "zero" solution and a "set-point" solution, and assumes "linearity" between the measurement response and the analyte concentration. "Multi-point calibration" is required for methods that do not generate a linear response (e.g., immunoassay methods) and usually involves analyzing three to five calibrator solutions and utilizing a curve-fitting routine to establish the calibration function. Methods may require calibration with each analytical run, or only daily, weekly, monthly, or even longer intervals, or only when a new lot of reagents are put into use, depending on the manufacturer's documentation of method stability.

Given that calibration determines the accuracy of test results, given that the accuracy of both two-point and multi-point calibration depends on the concentration range for which the calibration function is reliable, and given that method stability varies from one analytical system to another, it is important that laboratories periodically verify the correctness of the calibration function. That's the intent of the "calibration verification" in the Final CLIA Rule [1].

CLIA Rules for Calibration and Calibration Verification

The standard for calibration and calibration verification procedures begins as follows:

§493.1255 Calibration and calibration verification procedures are required to substantiate the continued accuracy of the test system throughout the laboratory's reportable range of test results for the test system.

Rules for calibration

§493.1255 (a) Perform and document calibration procedures –

(1) Following the manufacturer's test system instructions, using calibration materials provided or specified, and with at least the frequency recommended by the manufacturer;

(2) Using criteria verified or established by the laboratory as specified in 493.1253(b)(3) –

(i) Using calibration materials appropriate for the test system and, if possible, traceable to a reference method or reference material of known value;

(ii) Including the number, type, and concentration of calibration materials, as well as acceptable limits for and the frequency of calibration; and

(3) Whenever calibration verification fails to meet the laboratory's acceptable limits for calibration verification.

In short, this means that laboratories must follow the manufacturer's directions for calibration, re-calibrate as frequently as recommended by the manufacturer, plus re-calibrate whenever calibration verification fails.

Rules for calibration verification

§493.1255 (b) Perform and document calibration verification procedures -

(1) Following the manufacturer's calibration verification instructions:

(2) Using criteria verified or established by the laboratory under 493.1253(b)(3) –

(i) Including the number, type, and concentration of the materials, as well as acceptable limits for calibration verification; and

(ii) Including at least a minimal (or zero) value, a mid-point value, and a maximum value near the upper limit of the range to verify the laboratory's reportable range of test results for the test system; and

(3) At least once every 6 months and whenever any of the following occur:

(i) A complete change of reagents for a procedure is introduced, unless the laboratory can demonstrate that changing reagent lot numbers does not affect the range used to report patient test results, and control values are not adversely affected by reagent lot number changes.

(ii) There is major preventive maintenance or replacement of critical parts that may influence test performance.

(iii) Control materials reflect an unusual trend or shift, or are outside of the laboratory's acceptable limits, and other means of assessing and correcting unacceptable control values fail to identify and correct the problem.

(iv) The laboratory's established schedule for verifying the reportable range for patient test results requires more frequent calibration verification.

In short, this means that laboratories must either verify the calibration, or re-calibrate, at least every 6 months, after a change in reagents, after major preventive maintenance, after replacement of any major components, and anytime there is a quality control problem.

Definitions of terms

The Final CLIA Rule [1] includes the following definitions (493.2) that are important in interpreting these requirements:

> ***Calibration*** means a process of testing and adjusting an instrument or test system to establish a correlation between the measurement response and the concentration or amount of the substance that is being measured by the test procedure.

> ***Calibration verification*** means the assaying of materials of known concentration in the same manner as patient samples to substantiate the instrument or test system's calibration throughout the reportable range for patient test results.

Note the relationship to the "reportable range," which is also defined in the Final CLIA Rule [1], as follows:

> ***Reportable range*** means the span of test result values over which the laboratory can establish or verify the accuracy of the instrument or test system measurements response.

The College of American Pathologists takes a different view of calibration verification and does not require that it verify the reportable range of the method, which they also redefine into two new terms (December 2003 Laboratory General Checklist, Gen.42161):

> ***CAP Analytical measurement range (AMR)*** is the range of analyte values that a method can directly measure on the specimen without any dilution, concentration or other pretreatment not part of the usual assay process.

> ***CAP Clinically reportable range (CRR)*** is the range of analyte values that a method can measure, allowing for specimen dilution, concentration, or other pretreatment used to extend the direct analytical measurement range.

The CAP perspective on calibration verification is given in the December 2003 Chemistry and Toxicology Checklist, as follows:

> *Calibration of a test method, calibration verification, and validation of the analytical measurement range (AMR) are required to substantiate the continued accuracy of the method. For affected laboratories, the U.S. CLIA-88 regulations, revised January 2003, use the term 'calibration verification' to refer to both the verification of correct method calibration and validation of the reportable range,*

referred to here as AMR. This checklist uses separate terms (calibration verification and AMR) to identify two distinct processes that are required for good laboratory practice.

CAP Calibration: *The set of operations that establish, under specified conditions, the relationship between reagent system/ instrument response and the corresponding concentration/activity values of an analyte. Calibration procedures are typically specified by a method manufacturer, but may also be established by the laboratory.*

CAP Calibration verification: *The process of confirming that the current calibration settings remain valid for a method. If calibration verification confirms that the current calibration settings are valid, it is not necessary to perform a complete calibration or recalibration of the method.*

The CAP refinements allow calibration verification to be performed more simply, e.g., by running the calibrators as unknown samples, but then require that AMR be verified every 6 months. It is also possible to do both at once by analyzing at least 3 materials that are in the low, middle, and high parts of the reportable range or analytical measurement range.

Issues and Answers

What's the difference between calibration and calibration verification?

Calibration is typically performed using materials supplied by the manufacturer intended for that specific use. That might be just one calibrator or it could be a series of many calibrators. It is generally recommended that calibration verification employ *different* materials to provide an independent check on the adequacy of calibration, but CAP has also suggested that the original calibrators can be analyzed as unknowns, just like patient samples, to confirm correct values are obtained. For stable systems that are calibrated infrequently, CLIA requires verification of the calibration every 6 months

How is calibration performed?

You should follow the manufacturer's directions and use the calibrators supplied or recommended for this purpose. The performance characteristics of most methods are critically dependent on proper calibration, therefore manufacturers must be very careful in defining the calibration procedure. Laboratory users should follow those directions if they expect to achieve the performance claimed by the manufacturer. If you modify the method, for example, you become responsible for establishing the proper calibration procedure.

- Appendix C of the State Operations Manual [3] **D5425** states that *in establishing the calibration and quality control frequency, the laboratory must consider;*
  - ❍ *Test system instrument/reagent stability, including relocation;*
  - ❍ *Frequency with which the test is performed;*
  - ❍ *Technique dependence of the method;*
  - ❍ *Frequency of quality control failures; and*
  - ❍ *Training, experience, and competency of technical personnel.*

Again, it makes sense to operate the method as recommended by the manufacturer and be able to use the manufacturer's recommended calibration procedure.

When should calibration be performed?

According to the CLIA rules, a method should be calibrated whenever the manufacturer says so, whenever there is a complete change of reagents (unless QC results can document stability), whenever there is a major preventive maintenance or a replacement of critical parts that influence test performance, or whenever controls show an unusual trend or shift (and cannot be corrected by other means).

- **D5437** also notes that *if calibration proves less stable than the manufacturer's recommendation, additional calibration materials and/or more frequent calibration may be required...*

- **D5437** suggests only one *Probe*: *If the laboratory calculates values for one or more calibration materials, are the calculations correct,* *and do the records reflect that the measured values are within the laboratory's established limits for the calibration materials?*

When should calibration verification be performed?

At least every six months, if a method is calibrated less frequently or if it is calibrated with only 1 or 2 materials. However, if methods use 3 or more calibrators and are calibrated daily, weekly, or monthly, they don't require verification of calibration.

- **D5439.** *If the laboratory performs a calibration protocol using 3 or more levels of calibration materials that include a low, mid, and high value at least every 6 months, the calibration verification requirement is met.*
- **D5439** *Probe: If a laboratory does not perform calibration verification after a complete change of reagents, what data does the laboratory have to document that changing reagent lot numbers does not affect the reportable range of patient test results, and does not adversely affect control results?* This suggests that the laboratory could use its QC results to demonstrate that there hasn't been any change in performance due to a change of reagents.

How is calibration verification performed?

The laboratory should analyze at least 3 materials having known values, including a minimal or zero value, a mid-point value, and a maximum value near the upper limit of the reportable range. Calibration verification requires that the observed results for the materials agree with the known values within limits defined by the laboratory.

- **D5439** identifies appropriate materials as being calibration materials, proficiency testing samples with known results, or control materials with known values. *For these materials the laboratory must define acceptable limits for the difference between the measured value obtained, versus the actual concentration of the materials.*

Many manufacturers supply both calibrators and calibration verifiers for their systems. The calibrator verification materials may include more than 3 levels of concentration and may be designed to verify the manufacturer's claimed reportable range.

How are acceptable limits established?

Truth be told, the laboratory is free to do whatever it wants! However, it would be best that the laboratory director or clinical consultant sign-off on whatever limits are set. In general, laboratory quality management practices are not based on objective quality goals or performance criteria. But they could be! Given that CLIA defines minimum criteria for acceptable performance in proficiency testing surveys, one logical approach would be to utilize those criteria as minimum requirements for routine performance as well.

For example, if cholesterol is supposed to be correct to within 10% for PT, it certainly makes sense that that the limits for calibration verification not exceed 10%. It makes even more sense to set the acceptable limits tighter, say half to a third of the PT criteria, in consideration of the imprecision (random error) that is expected in every test result. If the systematic error due to calibration error consumes the entire CLIA allowable total error, then many patient test results will surely have larger errors due to the combined inaccuracy and imprecision of the method.

The CAP linearity survey program employs a similar approach, but includes a second criterion at the low end of the range (near the zero point) that is defined in concentration units, rather than as a percentage. With a percentage criterion, the acceptable limits at zero concentration would be zero, which is unrealistic. Therefore, CAP employs a percentage criterion at high concentrations and a fixed concentration criterion at the zero end of the analytical range.

What's the difference between the CLIA calibration verification and the CAP AMR verification procedures?

The CAP requirement for AMR verification is essentially the same as the CLIA requirement for calibration verification. If you find this confusing, you're not alone. It caused a lot of discussion when we wrote this chapter and we expect it will remain an area of confusion for some months and maybe years. We advise you to think about the CLIA requirement to validate reportable range as part of the initial validation of a method and not confuse that step with calibration verification. The test materials for the reportable range experiment could be dilutions or mixtures of fresh patient specimens without well-defined values. Think about calibration verification as a periodic check on the method accuracy using at least 3 materials having well-defined or known concentrations.

DO's and DON'Ts

- DO develop a list of your laboratory methods that have calibration intervals longer than 6 months and methods that use fewer than 3 calibration materials. Those are the ones that need verification at 6 month intervals.
- DO verify calibration when there are changes and problems occurring with the analytical methods and systems. This may be required after routine changes in reagent lots, major maintenance or replacement of critical components, system breakdowns and QC problems.
- DO run controls whenever changes occur with the analytical system in order to document that those changes haven't caused a change in method performance. While CLIA is most concerned about any effects on reportable range, it is also possible that system changes might affect precision or accuracy. Your QC will be helpful in picking up those problems.
- DON'T perform 6 month calibration verification for all of your methods. Those that are calibrated frequently using 3 or more materials do not require the 6 month verification.

References

1. US Centers for Medicare & Medicaid Services (CMS). Medicare, Medicaid, and CLIA Programs: Laboratory Requirements Relating to quality Systems and Certain Personnel Qualifications. Final Rule. Fed Regist Jan 24 2003;16:3640-3714.

2. CAP Laboratory Accreditation Checklists. http://www.cap.org/apps/docs/laboratory accreditation/checklists/checklistftp.html

3. CMS State Operations Manual – Interpretive Guidelines: Appendix C. www.cms.gov/clia/appendc.asp

9: Method Validation Data Analysis Tools

One of the major difficulties that laboratories encounter with method validation is data analysis. What do you do with all the data? It's easy to perform statistical calculations today, but *which* calculations should you perform and what should you do with the results?

There are absolutely no guidelines for data analysis in the CLIA regulations or the State Operations Manual. Likewise, there is little guidance available in the checklists and standards from CAP and JCAHO. One might conclude that it doesn't make any difference what laboratories do with the data as long as they calculate some statistics, prepare some graphs, and have those results available to show the inspector. And the truth is, that probably will be sufficient to demonstrate the laboratory has attempted to validate the performance of the method.

It would be better, of course, to have a rational approach for selecting the statistical calculations and graphical analyses that are appropriate and useful. That's the purpose of this chapter.

What's the problem with statistics?

Actually, the problem has to do with people being confused by statistics. Just mention the word "statistics" and many people have a psychological block and are unable to think any further about the data and what it means. And the situation is confounded by common practices where statistics are misused.

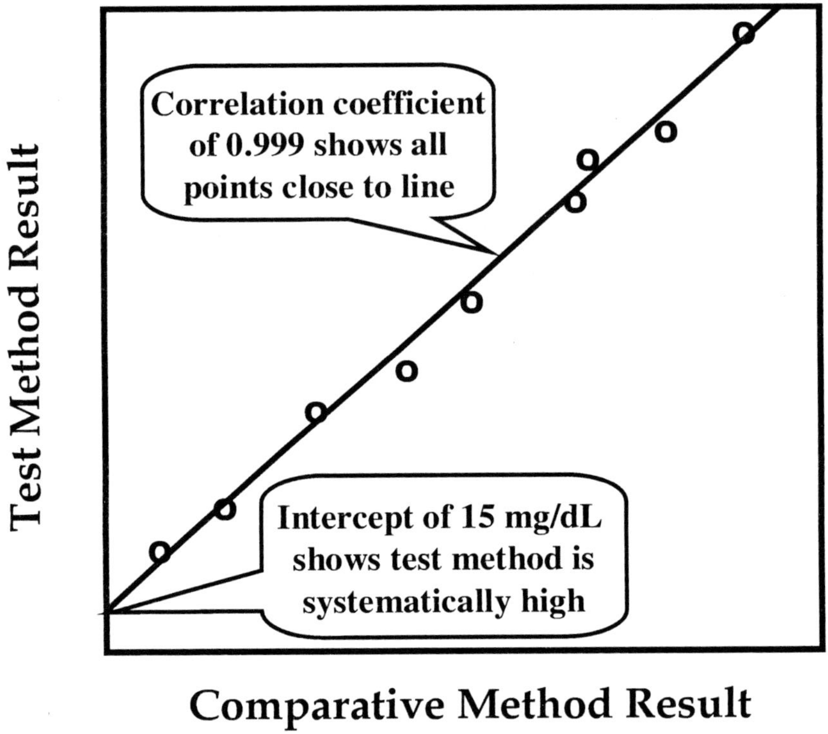

The figure here shows data from a comparison of methods experiment, where the results from the new method are shown on the y-axis versus the results of the comparative method on the x-axis. These data provide a classical example where the correlation coefficient is 0.999, very close to the ideal or perfect value of 1.000, but the "line of best fit" shows a slope of 1.00 and a y-intercept of 15 mg/dL. Many people would interpret the correlation coefficient to mean there is nearly perfect agreement between the results of the new method and the comparative method. WRONG! The results by the new method are generally 15 mg/dL higher than the comparative method.

If this figure represented a glucose method, are the results by the new method acceptable? Would a laboratory provide satisfactory service if all patient results were 15 mg/dL high?

What are the secrets to better statistical analysis?

Here's how to make sense of the statistical analysis of data from method validation experiments. The process is simple once you understand what needs to be done. However, few people know the secrets to doing this right and that's why method validation is often done so poorly.

1. **It's all about errors!** That's the first and most important secret. The purpose is to collect data that will reveal the errors that are present in the test results from the method and the range over which the test results are expected to be reliable.

2. **Different experiments provide estimates of different errors!** Different experiments, such as replication, comparison of methods, and interference are used to determine different types of errors. Other experiments, such as reportable range and detection limit, are used to defined the analytical range over which those estimates of errors are reliable.

3. **Statistics are tools to estimate the errors!** The right statistics are the ones that help you estimate the size of the errors in the experimental data. Given that different experiments are used to estimate different errors, it is expected that there will be different statistics that are useful with different experiments. Likewise, different graphical presentations go along with the different statistics.

4. **Different statistics are sensitive to different types of errors!** It is particularly important to recognize which errors show up on which statistics in the method comparison experiment. While it is common to utilize the correlation coefficient, t-test statistics (bias, SDdiff, t-value), and regression statistics (slope, y-intercept, and standard error about the regression line), these statistics are not equal with respect to providing useful information.

5. **Statistical significance is not the same as clinical significance!** While it is common to use "tests of significance"

such a t-test and F-test, they are mainly useful for comparing the results in your laboratory with the claims made by the manufacturer. They can answer the question "are the laboratory's results any different from the performance claimed by the manufacturer?" However, that is not the same as judging whether or not performance is acceptable for patient care.

6. **Judgments on acceptability depend on the quality required for the test, i.e., clinical significance, not statistical significance!** The basic idea is to compare the errors observed for the method with the amount of error that is allowable for the test. If the observed errors are larger than what is allowable, the method is not acceptable. If the observed errors are smaller than what is allowable, the method is acceptable.

What types of analytical errors are of interest?

Since the data analysis is all about errors, it's important to understand the types of errors that may occur. Using the comparison of methods experiment again, the figure here shows the types of analytical errors that might occur – random and systematic. This figure expands the error model described earlier in Chapter 7 to include two types of systematic error.

- ***Random error, RE.*** An error that can be positive or negative, whose direction and exact magnitude cannot be exactly predicted.
- ***Constant systematic error, CE.*** An error that is always the same direction and magnitude even as the concentration of analyte changes.
- ***Proportional systematic error, PE.*** An error that is always the same direction and whose magnitude is a proportion or percentage of the concentration of the analyte being measured.

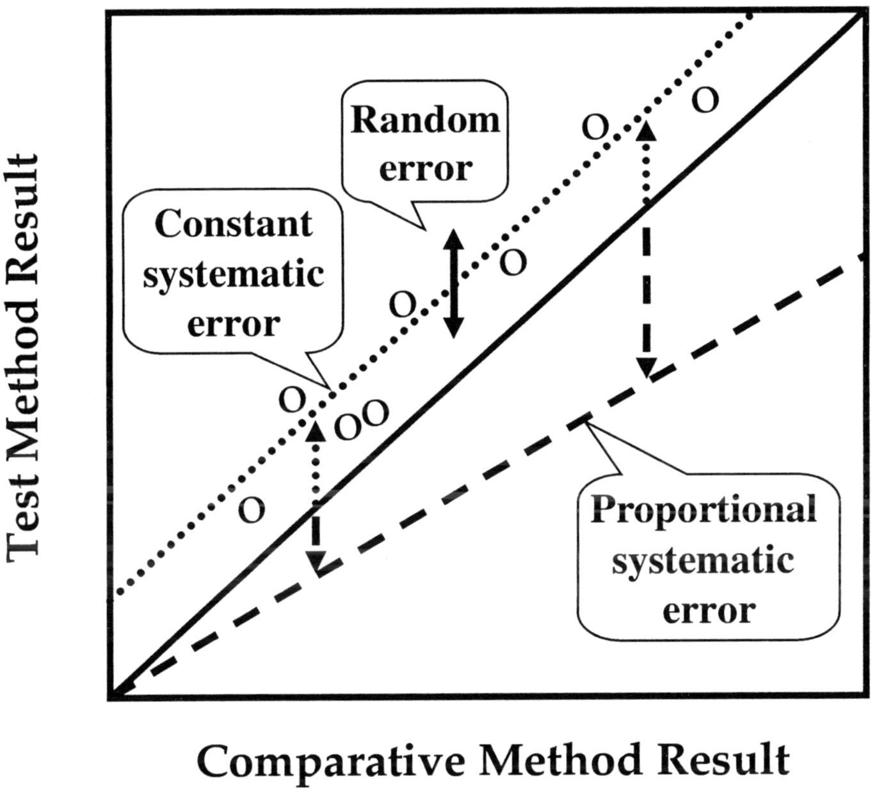

Random error is shown by the scatter in the data points about the dotted line. Constant systematic error is shown by the dotted line and its displacement from the ideal solid line. Note that the dotted line shows a uniform displacement through the concentration range, i.e., the same size error or constant error. In contrast, the dashed line shows proportional error, where the displacement increases as the concentration of the analyte increases, i.e., a proportional error.

How are different types of errors estimated?

Here's where the different method validation experiments become important. The replication experiment is used to estimate random error. A short time span, such as one day, leads to a "within day" estimate. A longer time span, such as 20 to 30 days, leads to a more reliable "day to day" estimate of "total" imprecision. Constant and proportional errors could be estimated from interference and recovery experiments, or can also be determined with a comparison of methods experiment. Remember that for unmodified non-waived FDA cleared methods, it is not necessary to perform interference and recovery experiments. However, if a laboratory makes any change to a method, then additional evaluation work is needed, including interference and recovery studies.

<table>
<tr><th rowspan="2">Type of Analytic Error</th><th colspan="2">Experiment</th></tr>
<tr><th>Preliminary</th><th>Final</th></tr>
<tr><td>Random Error</td><td>Replication Within run</td><td>Replication Between runs</td></tr>
<tr><td>Constant Error</td><td>Interference</td><td rowspan="2">Comparison of Methods</td></tr>
<tr><td>Proportional Error</td><td>Recovery</td></tr>
</table>

What calculation tools are available?

Given that different types of errors lead to different experiments which lead to different sets of data, now we have to consider how to perform the appropriate statistical calculations on those sets of data. The basic calculations needed are for means, SDs, regression statistics, t-test statistics, plus graphical displays.

Any scientific calculator can provide means, SDs, and regression analysis. Likewise, electronic spreadsheets such as Excel® include many standard statistical calculations and can be programmed to provide other calculations of interest. There also are statistical programs on personal computers, e.g., Minitab®, SAS, SPSS, etc., can provide a wide variety of statistical calculations and graphical presentations of the data. One concern with all these tools is that the statistical results still depend on the person, i.e., they assume the individual knows what they're doing and does it correctly. In our experience with students in the classroom, they are able to get quite a variety of answers (many of them incorrect) for a single set of data when using these tools.

There also are statistical programs that are specifically designed for method validation studies. This is by no means a complete list, but here are several that we know are available:

- ***Analyse-it*** is an add-on for the MicroSoft Excel® spreadsheet; available from Analyse-it Software, Ltd (www.analyse-it.com)
- ***CBStat*** is a PC program available from Kristian Linnet (www.cbstat.com).
- ***EP Evaluator*** provides an extensive list of modules that cover all the experiments and also the specific recommendations of the NCCLS protocols; available from David G. Rhoads Associates (www.dgrhoads.com).
- ***EP Suite*** from Robert Martin at Machem Associates (www.marchem.com)
- ***Method Validator*** is a PC program available from Philippe Marquis at Marquis-soft (www.marquis-soft.com).

What statistics and graphs are most useful?

One set of tools can be found on Westgard Web and will be used here to illustrate the data analysis process (www.westgard.com/mvtools.html). This toolkit is advantageous for educational purposes because it associates the right statistics and right graphics with the right experiments. It is also very easy to use with small data sets to explore the behavior of different statistics.

Here's a picture of the tool kit needed to analyze the data from basic method validation experiments. The tool kit includes several calculators and plotters:

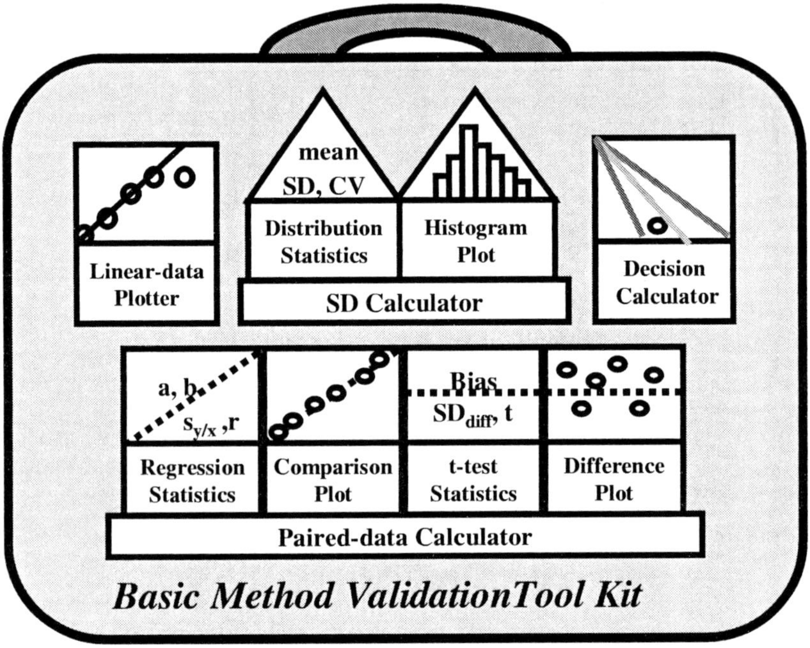

- **Linear data plotter** is used to determine the reportable range. It provides a display the observed method response versus the assigned concentrations for a series of solutions or specimens;
- **SD calculator** is used with data from the replication experiment to determine distribution statistics (mean, SD, and CV) and to display a histogram of the distribution;

- **Paired data calculator** is used with data from a comparison of methods experiment to determine regression statistics (slope or a, y-intercept or b, standard deviation about the regression line or $s_{y/x}$, and correlation coefficient, r), display the data in a comparison plot (test method as y, comparison method as x), determine t-test statistics (bias, SD_{diff}, and t-value), and display data in the form of a difference plot (y-x vs x);

- **Method decision calculator** is used to judge the acceptability of method performance. It makes use of the SD or CV calculated from replication data and/or the bias or systematic error estimated from the comparison of methods experiment.

These tools include both statistical calculations and graphical displays of the data. There is an association between certain calculations and certain graphs because they complement each other for describing and displaying a set of data. For example, distribution statistics are used with a histogram plot to display data for imprecision or random error. For inaccuracy or systematic error, regression statistics are used with a comparison plot; t-test statistics are used with a difference plot.

There is a natural order for using the tools, which is suggested by their location in the tool kit. Those at the top are generally pulled out first, e.g. the linear-data plotter is used in the beginning to establish the reportable range of the method, after which the SD calculator will be used to estimate the imprecision or random error, whose acceptability can be assessed using the decision calculator. After these steps, the paired-data calculator will be used to estimate the inaccuracy of the method and the decision calculator used again to assess the overall performance of the method.

How do you use these tools?

The **linear-data plotter** is used with the data collected in the linearity experiment, where the purpose is to assess the range over which patient results may be reported, i.e., reportable range. The response of the method is plotted on the y-axis versus the relative concentration or assigned values of the samples or specimens on the x-axis. The "reportable range" is generally estimated as the linear working range of the analytical method.

The **SD calculator** is used for the data collected in the replication experiment, where the objective is to estimate the random error or imprecision of the method on the basis of repeated measurements on the same sample material. The statistics that should be calculated are the mean, SD, and CV. Also be sure to record the number of measurements used in the calculations.

- The mean, or average of the group of results, describes the central location of the measurements.
- The SD describes the expected distribution of results, i.e., 66% are expected to be within ± 1 SD of the mean, 95% within ± 2 SD of the mean, and 99.7% within ± 3 SD of the mean.
- The CV, or coefficient of variation, is equal to the SD divided by the mean, times 100 to express in percent.
- The histogram displays the distribution of results. Ideally, the distribution should appear Gaussian, or "normal."

The **paired data calculator** may be used with the pairs of results on each specimen analyzed by the test and comparison methods in the comparison of methods experiment. This is the most complicated part of the statistical analysis and requires the most care and attention. Linear regression statistics may be used with a comparison plot, or t-test statistics may be used with a difference plot.

The regression statistics that should be calculated are the slope (b) and y-intercept of the line (a), the standard deviation of the points about that line ($s_{y/x}$), and the correlation coefficient (r, the Pearson product moment correlation coefficient). You may also see the slope designated as m, the y-intercept as b, and the standard deviation as $s_{residuals}$, respectively. The correlation coefficient is included to help you decide whether the linear regression statistics or the t-test statistics will provide the most reliable estimates of systematic error.

Sensitivity of Statistics	RE	CE	PE
Regression			
Slope, b	No	No	**Yes**
Y-intercept, a	No	**Yes**	No
SD about line, $s_{y/x}$	**Yes**	No	No
T-test			
Bias	No	**Yes**	*Yes?*
SDdiff	**Yes**	No	*Yes?*
Correlation coefficient			
r	*Yes?*	*No?*	*No?*

- The slope describes the angle of the line that provides the best fit to the test and comparison results. A perfect slope would be 1.00. Deviations from 1.00 are an indication of proportional systematic error [1].
- The y-intercept describes where the line of best fit intersects with the y-axis. Ideally, the y-intercept should be 0.0. Deviations from 0.0 are an indication of constant systematic error [1].
- The $s_{y/x}$ term describes the scatter of the data around the line of best fit. It provides an estimate of the random error between methods which includes both the imprecision of the test and comparison methods, as well as possible matrix effects that vary from one specimen to another. It will never be zero because both the test and comparison methods have some imprecision [1].
- The correlation coefficient describes how well the results between the two methods change together. An r of +1.00 indicates perfect correlation, i.e., all the points fall perfectly on a line that shows the test method values vs the comparison method values. Values less than 1.00 indicate there is scatter in the

data about the line of best fit. The lower the r value, the more scatter in the data. The main use of r is to help you assess the reliability of the linear regression calculations – **r should never be used as an indicator of method acceptability** [1]. When r is 0.99 or greater, linear regression calculations will provide reliable estimates of errors. When r is less than 0.975, it is better to use the paired data calculations or an alternate (and more complicated) regression technique such as Deming's regression [4,5].

- A comparison plot should be used to display the data from the comparison of methods experiment (plotting the comparison method value on the x-axis and the test method value on the y-axis). This plot is then used to visually inspect the data to identify possible outliers and to assess the range of linear agreement [1].

The t-test statistics of interest are the bias, SD of the differences, and lastly, something called a t-value which also requires knowledge of the number of paired sample measurements. Again, be sure to keep track of the number of measurements, which for the comparison of methods experiment is the number of patient specimens compared.

- The bias is the difference between the averages by the two methods, which is also the same as the average difference for all the specimens analyzed by the two methods. It provides an estimate of the systematic error or average difference that is expected between the methods – the smaller the bias, the smaller the systematic error, the better the agreement.

- The SD of the differences provides an estimate of the random error between the methods. It will never be zero because both the test and comparison methods have some imprecision.

- The t-value itself is an indicator of whether enough paired sample measurements have been collected to know whether the observed bias is real, or statistically significant. As a rule of thumb, in a method comparison experiment where the minimum of 40 patient specimens have been compared, if t is greater than 2.0, the data is sufficient to conclude that a bias exists. It's important to note that it's the size of the bias that's important in judging the acceptability of the method, not the size of the t-value.

- A difference plot should be used to display the differences between paired results, plotting the difference between the test method minus comparison method values on the y-axis versus the comparison method result on the x-axis. Difference plots are being popularized today because of their simplicity [6], however, their use and interpretation are not so simple when you want to make a quantitative and objective decision about method performance [7].

The **decision calculator** is used to display the estimates of random and systematic errors and judge the performance of the method [3]. Therefore, this chart depends on the estimates of errors that are obtained from other statistical calculations. In brief, the chart is drawn on the basis of the quality requirement that is defined for the method and shows the allowable inaccuracy on the y-axis versus the allowable imprecision on the x-axis. The observed imprecision and inaccuracy of the method are then plotted to display the method's "operating point" (y-coordinate is the estimate of inaccuracy or SE, x-coordinate is the estimate of imprecision or RE). The position of this operating point is interpreted relative to the lines that define areas of "unacceptable", "poor," "marginal," "good," "excellent", and "world class" performance. We will discuss this further in the next chapter.

Issues and Answers

What statistics should be used for reportable range?

Here's where graphical analysis is still considered to be the "gold standard." Plot the observed results on the y-axis versus the expected results (known, bottle value) on the x-axis. Draw the best straight line through the data points, paying most attention to the data points on the lower half of the range rather than the upper half of the range. Estimate the upper limit of the reportable range as the concentration where the data points start to deviate from the line.

How can a manufacturer's claim for precision be verified?

Use the data from a replication experiment and calculate the mean, SD, and CV. Then compare the observed SD or CV with the one claimed by the manufacturer. If your observed SD or CV is smaller than the manufacturer's claim, you have verified the claim. If your observed SD or CV is larger than the manufacturer's claim, calculate an F-value from the equation $F_{calc} = SD_{larger}^2/SD_{smaller}^2$. For example, if the observed SD were 4 and the manufacturer's claim was 3, then F_{calc} is 16/9 or 1.78. To assess whether the difference is statistically significant, compare the calculated F-value to the critical F-value (which is found in a statistical table). In the typical case where 21 replicate measurements have been made by both the manufacturer and the user, the critical F is 2.12. If the calculated F is smaller than the critical F, there is no statistically significant difference, i.e., the observed SD of 4 is not really different from the manufacturer's value of 3 based on the amount of data included in the estimates.

How can a manufacturer's claim for accuracy be verified?

If you happen to employ the same comparative method as the manufacturer, then you can use your data from the comparison of methods experiment together with t-test analysis. The bias term will be the best estimate of systematic error at the mean of the comparison data. If bias is zero, then there is no difference between the two methods. If bias is a finite number, then you can use the calculated t-value to determine whether the bias is really different from zero. If the calculated t-value is less than the critical t-value (obtained from a statistical table), then there is no statistically significant difference, i.e., no real difference between the two methods based on the amount of data collected.

If you employ a different comparative method (from that used by the manufacturer), then the t-test would only show whether there is a difference between the new method and your comparative method, which may or may not be represent the true or correct values for the test.

Why can't the correlation coefficient be used to validate accuracy?

The correlation coefficient, r, is widely used with data from the comparison of methods experiment, but does not provide any estimate of systematic error, which is the purpose of that experiment. The table shown on page 99 summarizes the response of different statistics to different types of analytical errors in data from a comparison of methods experiment. The slope from regression will provide an estimate of proportional systematic error and the y-intercept an estimate of constant systematic error. In t-test statistics, the bias will provide an estimate of the combined effects of proportional and systematic errors. *Note that the correlation coefficient does NOT respond to either proportional or systematic error, therefore it does not provide any measure of accuracy!*

The only practical value of the correlation coefficient is to provide an indicator for the **reliability** of the regression statistics. If r is high, it means that the comparison data covers a wide analytical range and therefore should provide reliable estimates of the slope and intercept. One recommendation is that an r of 0.975 or greater indicates that simple linear regression will be reliable [8]. For lower values of r, it is recommended that additional data be collected to expand the range covered, or alternative statistical techniques be used, such as Deming regression or Passing-Bablock regression, or possibly t-test statistics if the mean of the patient data is close to the decision level of interest [9].

What is Bland-Altman analysis?

Bland and Altman are two scientists who have recommended the use of t-test statistics and a difference plot to analyze data from a comparison of methods experiment [10]. There is one special wrinkle with the Bland-Altman difference plot – they recommend that the value on the x-axis be the *average of the values* from the test and comparison methods. The value on the y-axis is the difference between the test and comparison values. In effect, this difference plot magnifies the scatter of the data or the random error between the two methods. The main argument for using Bland-Altman analysis is that people don't know how to use regression statistics properly. However, our recommendation is to first try regression analysis and check the correlation coefficient to see if the slope and intercept are reliable. If the regression statistics are reliable, calculate the systematic errors as discussed below. If not reliable, then use bias from t-test statistics as the estimate of systematic error or accuracy.

How is method inaccuracy or systematic error calculated from regression statistics?

Remember that regression statistics give you the slope (b) and y-intercept (a) for the best straight line through the comparison of methods data. Select an important decision concentration, X_c, then use the regression equation to calculate the corresponding Y_c value. The difference between $Y_c - X_c$ is the best estimate of systematic error at that concentration.

Here's an example for a cholesterol test, where the slope=0.97 and the y-intercept=1.0 mg/dL. At a concentration of 200 mg/dL where test interpretation is critical, the expected result from the test method is given by $Y_c = a + bX_c$, which is 195 mg/dL [1.0 + 0.97*200]. The difference between Y_c and X_c is 5 mg/dL (195 – 200), which is the best estimate of systematic error at a concentration of 200 mg/dL. You can also expect the bias term from t-test statistics will be close to 5 mg/dL if the mean of the patient values is close to the decision level concentration of 200 mg/dL.

How can reference intervals be transferred using regression statistics?

Perform the same calculations as shown above ($Y_c = a + bX_c$) to determine the Y values that correspond to the upper and lower limits of the reference interval, i.e., calculate Y first for X_{upper} and then for X_{lower}. The corresponding Y_{upper} and Y_{lower} values represent the limits of the reference interval for the new method.

Can detection limit be calculated using the Westgard Web Internet tools?

The detection limit can be estimated from a replication experiment, where the specimen is chosen to have a zero or very low concentration.

The data calculations should provide estimates of the mean and SD. The CV is of limited value because the mean is so low. Detection limit should be expressed in concentration units, usually as the mean value + 2 SD or sometimes the mean value + 3 SD.

Can interference be calculated using these Internet tools?

Interference experiments typically involve pairs of samples, one containing the suspected interference and the other representing the same specimen without interference. These paired results can be evaluated using the paired-data calculator, where bias will represent the average interference observed for the specimens tested.

DOs and DON'Ts

- DO utilize graphs to view and display your data. They make it easy to see "funny" points which need to be investigated further.
- DO inspect the data being collected in real time so any problems can be investigated while the specimens are still available. It's much better to resolve outliers first rather than trying to compensate for them later in the data analysis.
- DO select the right data analysis tools for each experiment and set of data. There is no value to calculating miscellaneous statistics just to have printouts in your files. The wrong statistics may confuse rather than clarify the meaning of the data.
- DON'T depend on the correlation coefficient as a measure of accuracy. It's mainly useful as an indicator of the reliability of the slope and intercept from regression analysis.
- DON'T depend on t-test statistics or Bland-Altman analysis for an estimate of systematic error for medical decision levels away from the mean of the patient data.
- DON'T make any decision on method acceptability based on the correlation coefficient, t-test, or F-test. Statistical significance is not the same as clinical significance. Clinical significance is

judged by comparing the size of the errors observed with the amount of error that would be allowable without compromising the clinical use and interpretation of the test results.

- DO check the assumptions for reliability of the data analysis. For regression analysis, inspect the comparison plot for linearity, wide analytical range, and outliers. For t-test analysis, inspect the difference plot for outliers and uniformity of scatter through the analytical range.

References

1. Westgard JO, Hunt MR. Use and interpretation of common statistical tests in method comparison studies. Clin Chem 1973;19:49-57.
2. Westgard JO, Carey RN, Wold S. Criteria for judging precision and accuracy in method development and evaluation. Clin Chem 1974;20:825-33.
3. Westgard JO. A method evaluation decision chart (MEDx Chart) for judging method performance. Clin Lab Science. 1995;8:277-83.
4. Stockl D, Dewitte K, Thienpont M. Validity of linear regression in method comparison studies: limited by the statistical model or the quality of the analytical data? Clin Chem 1998;44:2340-6.
5. Cornbleet PJ, Gochman N. Incorrect least-squares regression coefficients in method-comparison analysis. Clin Chem 1979;25:432-8.
6. Bland JM, Altman DG. Statistical methods for assessing agreement beween two methods of clinical measurement. Lancet 1986;307-10.
7. Hyltoft Petersen P, Stockl D, Blaabjerg O, Pedersen B, Birkemose E, Thienpont L, Flensted Lassen J, Kjeldsen J. Graphical interpretration of analytical data from comparison of a field method with a reference method by use of difference plots [opinion]. Clin Chem 1997;43:2039-46.
8. Westgard JO. Points of care in using statistics in method comparison studies. Clin Chem 1998;44:2240-2242.
9. Bland JM, Altman DG. Statistical methods for assessing agreement between two methods of clinical measurement. Lancet 1986;i:307-310.

10: Analytical Quality Assessment

Chapter 9 provides some guidance for improving the statistical analysis of method validation data, but it doesn't provide an answer to the question "Is method performance acceptable?" That's the purpose of this chapter.

CLIA doesn't actually require a laboratory to make sure method performance is acceptable, only to verify a manufacturer's claims for performance. All manufacturers are required to establish the precision and accuracy of their analytical systems in order to gain FDA approval for the introduction of new methods. The clause "unmodified FDA-cleared or approved test system" in §493.1253 refers to a method that has been approved via the FDA 510K review of a manufacturer's labeling claims. Any analytical system on the market should have passed the FDA approval process, which means there are labeling claims for precision, accuracy, reportable range, reference intervals, detection limit (if applicable), interferences, and possibly QC instructions.

Note, however, there is no claim that method performance will meet the needs and requirements for medical care. The FDA 510K approval process does NOT require any claim for quality. The FDA only reviews a manufacturer's data to be sure the performance claims are consistent with the data. It is perfectly legal and entirely possible that a manufacturer may claim performance that is not medically useful!

We believe that the laboratory has a responsibility to go further than required by CLIA if it wants to assure that testing satisfies the medical needs of its physicians and patients. This can be done by evaluating method performance data relative to some defined standard of quality. Is a CV of 3.0% adequate for patient care? Is a bias of 2.0% low enough to minimize any problems in patient care? Is the method's total error small enough to allow proper interpretation of test results according to clinical treatment guidelines?

CLIA minimum requirements for analytical quality

CLIA actually defines minimum requirements for analytical quality for approximately 80 different tests by the criteria for acceptable performance in proficiency testing. These requirements are summarized in Appendix 1 of this book.

For cholesterol, the requirement is stated as "Target value ± 10%." This means that at a concentration of 200 mg/dL (example target value, TV), the allowable error is 20 mg/dL. This is the error that is allowable in a single measurement of a cholesterol sample, therefore it might be composed of random error and/or systematic error, which means it is best thought of as a Total Allowable Error (TE_a).

For some tests, there are two criteria given. For example, for glucose, acceptable performance is defined as "Target value ± 6 mg/dL or ± 10% (greater)." This means that at a medical decision level of 50 mg/dL, the greater or larger number would be the 6 mg/dL, which corresponds to 12%. At a medical decision level of 125 mg/dL, the greater or larger number is 10%, or 12.5 mg/dL.

For some tests, particularly those in endocrinology and general immunology, the criteria are given as "Target value ± 3 SD." The SD here refers to the variation observed for the group of laboratories that participate in a proficiency testing event. In effect, this is a "state of the art" criterion – the lab should be as good as most other laboratories who perform this test. Criteria of this form can also be evaluated using data from peer-review programs, where laboratories voluntarily participate in testing the same materials, usually QC materials.

Thus, there are default standards for minimum analytical quality in the CLIA regulations themselves. Even though manufacturers make no claim for quality, CLIA has certain minimum requirements that must be achieved.

A Sigma Metric for Analytical Quality

Healthcare organizations have begun to adopt Six Sigma[1] because it offers real hope for improving quality management thinking and processes. The reason is that Six Sigma focuses on defects, which in turn requires that goals or requirements for good quality be defined.

The name "Six Sigma" comes from the goal that is being set for process performance. As shown in this figure, six sigmas or standard deviations of method variation should fit within the tolerance specifications for the product or process. The term "tolerance specifications" can be equated with the quality requirement from the CLIA regulations, i.e., a test is supposed to be correct within certain tolerances.

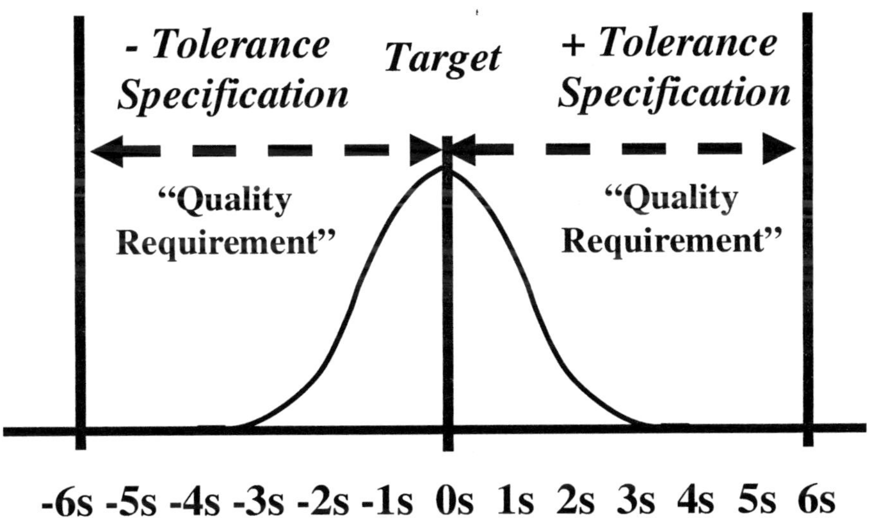

Six Sigma provides a universal methodology for measuring quality by counting the defects, determining the defect rate as "defects per million" or "DPM," and then converting DPM to a Sigma metric (by use of standard tables available in any Six Sigma text). Benchmarking can be done using the Sigma metrics, which account for the quality required for any product or process and allow universal comparisons across services and industries. See appendices 2 and 3 for more explanation about this topic.

For laboratory testing methods, it is possible to predict the performance of analytical testing processes based on estimates of the precision and accuracy of a method. Given that CLIA requires a laboratory to have these estimates for any methods implemented after April 24, 2003, it should be easy to utilize Six Sigma concepts and metrics to evaluate performance.

The calculation is very simple:

$$\textbf{Sigma} = (\textbf{TE}_a - \textbf{bias})/\textbf{CV}$$

- where TE_a is the CLIA quality requirement for acceptable performance in proficiency testing,
- bias is the estimate of systematic error from a comparison of methods experiment, and
- CV is the estimate of random error or imprecision from a replication experiment.

As an example, for a cholesterol method shown in the accompanying figure, given that the CLIA minimum requirement for quality is 10%, method bias is 1%, and the method CV is 2.0%, the method has 4.5 Sigma performance [(10-1)/2].

Calculation of Method Sigma

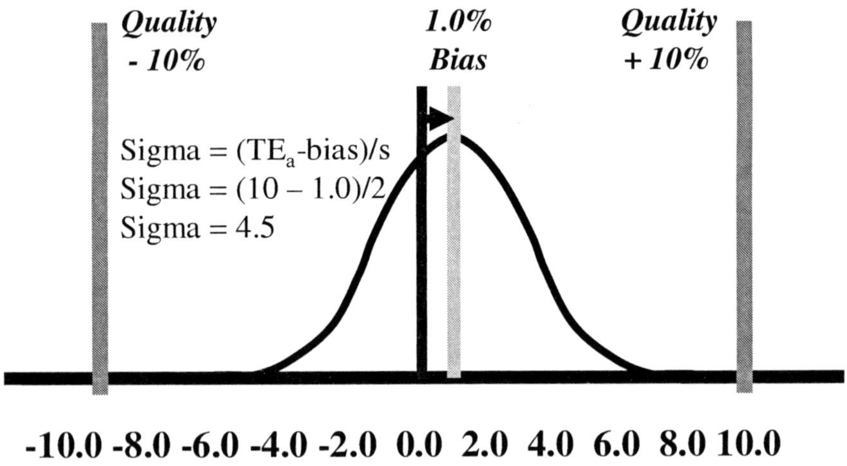

Note of clarification about terms and units: All the terms in the equation must be in the same units, either concentration units or units of percent. Given that the CLIA values for TE_a are most often given in percent, the bias and SD (or s) can be expressed as percentages by dividing the concentration values by a critical medical decision concentration. For SD or s, the corresponding percentage term is the Coefficient of Variation, CV. For bias, there is no separate term to express bias as a percent, but it would be calculated in the same way as a CV, e.g., 2 mg/dL divide by 200 mg/dL or 1.0% bias. As long as units are the same, the Sigma metric will also come out the same.

Sigma performance benchmarks

In interpreting the Sigma metric of a method, remember that the higher the Sigma value, the better the method performance. Established performance benchmarks are as follows:

- 6.0 Sigma is the goal for world class quality;
- 5.0 Sigma is the initial goal for process improvement;
- 4.0 Sigma is thought to be the average performance of current business and industrial processes;
- 3.0 Sigma is the minimum allowable Sigma for routine production.

For comparison purposes, airline baggage handling is generally quoted as 4.15 Sigma performance. On the other hand, airline safety is better than 6 Sigma. Everyone has experienced processes with these levels of performance, therefore, everyone including our patients can understand quality on the Sigma scale. Nevalainen et al [2] studied the performance of 12 different laboratory processes, mainly pre-analytic and post-analytic, and observed Sigma metrics from 2.20 to 4.80, with an average of 3.65 Sigma performance, thus laboratory processes have similar quality to typical business processes. That also means there is considerable room for improvement!

Some example calculations

Cholesterol. According to the National Cholesterol Education Program, a cholesterol method should have a CV of 3.0% or better and a bias of 3% or better. Given the CLIA minimum requirement that cholesterol should be correct to within 10%, how much better?

(A) Sigma = [(10-3)/3] = 2.33 if the method just satisfies the NCEP specifications; not good enough for production!

(B) Sigma = [(10-0)/3] = 3.33 if the method bias can be eliminated; minimum performance to go into production!

(C) Sigma = [(10-0)/2] = 5.0 if the method CV can be improved to 2.0%; that's the real goal for easy management of the cholesterol test in the laboratory.

(D) To achieve 6 Sigma performance, the method bias must be 0.0% and the method CV 1.7%.

Tests in a regional reference laboratory. Sigma metrics were calculated for 37 different tests that represented high volume automated operations [1]. The Sigma metrics ranged from 10.0 to 1.67. Eleven tests performed at the 6 Sigma level or better; another fourteen tests performed between 4 Sigma and 6 Sigma; six tests performed between 3 and 4 Sigma; and six tests performed at less than 3 Sigma. You can expect to encounter a similar mix in your lab: some of the tests will show high Sigma performance, some will show acceptable performance, and some will need care and attention.

Issues and Answers

What are the advantages and disadvantages of using a predictive measure, rather than actually counting the defects?

The advantage of calculating a Sigma metric directly from the observed bias and variation is that it is much quicker and easier to do. Imagine trying to inspect several thousand test results to determine which are defective! We have the data for estimating precision and accuracy available, first from the initial method validation studies and later from ongoing QC and peer-comparison or proficiency test surveys. The disadvantage is that we make an assumption that performance is stable and will remain this way. To guard against changes in performance, i.e., instability of a method over time, it is necessary to perform the appropriate QC. The QC itself should be designed around the same quality requirement and observed method performance in order to detect medically important changes. See Chapter 14 for more guidance on doing the appropriate QC.

How can the Sigma metric be calculated from a manufacturer's claims?

The starting point is to look up the CLIA requirement for acceptable performance. Next decide on the concentration level where the test results are most critically interpreted. Look at the manufacturer's precision claims and select an estimate that represents day-to-day performance closest to the decision level of interest. Then look carefully at how the manufacturer makes the claim for accuracy. Often that claim shows the statistical summary of comparison of methods data. If regression statistics are used, calculate the systematic error at the critical medical decision level (see Chapter 9). Be sure to express the estimate of precision and accuracy in the same units as the quality requirement, then calculate the Sigma metric.

Why don't manufacturers make a claim for quality and provide the Sigma metric for method performance?

One reason is that the FDA doesn't require a claim for quality. While FDA, CMS, and CDC work together to implement the laboratory regulations, they each have their own agendas and interests. CDC most likely generated the CLIA requirements for acceptable performance, but doesn't have anything to do with the application of those requirements either through the inspection of laboratories or the review of manufacturer's products. CMS is responsible for laboratory inspections, but has limited interaction with manufacturers. FDA is responsible for review of manufacturer's products and is guided by the principle of "truth in labeling." Thus it remains for the laboratory to take responsibility for assuring the necessary quality is being provided for the patients being served. There also is another important reason why this responsibility should be assumed by the laboratory rather than the manufacturer – the quality required for patient testing may vary from one laboratory to another based on the patients being served (e.g., transplant hospital vs physician's office laboratory).

What estimate of precision is best for calculating the Sigma metric?

The Sigma metric will undoubtedly be better (higher) if the precision estimate comes from a short time period, especially if it were within run. However, it is better to use the typical day-to-day estimate from 20 or 30 days. That is more representative of the performance that will be experienced over time.

What estimate of bias is best for calculating the Sigma metric?

The actual value of the bias may vary depending on how it is estimated. For example, if the bias is taken from the initial comparison of methods experiment, it will depend on technical characteristics and analytical quality of the comparative method. If taken from a peer-comparison program where there are subgroups for each instrument, the estimate of bias will tend to be low or optimistic. One approach for assessing the effect of the bias estimate itself is to calculate the Sigma metric with a bias of zero for comparison purposes. The Sigma metric will be at its optimum if bias is considered to be zero.

Are there other sources of recommendations for allowable total errors?

There is a large list of recommendations that are based on biologic variation that have been collated by Ricos et al [3]. This data bank is updated approximately once a year and is available on Westgard Web at (www.westgard.com/biodatabase1.htm). There also is an extensive compilation in Fraser's book on Biological Variation [4], which is available through AACC.

Aren't there other more practical goals for performance than Six Sigma?

Historically, recommendations began with 2 Sigma performance in 1974 [5], 3 Sigma performance in 1990 [6], and 4 Sigma performance in 1990 [7], leading up to the goal of 6 Sigma performance in 2001 [1]. All of these performance goals can be incorporated in the "method decision chart" that characterizes performance as unacceptable, poor, marginal, good, excellent, and world class [8].

How do you prepare a method decision chart?

The method decision chart illustrates the Sigma performance by plotting a point that represents the bias and CV observed for the method. Here are the step-by-step directions for preparing the chart, plus an example that shows the chart for a cholesterol test.

(or, Download it at www.westgard.com/SixSigmaMEDX.html)

1. First define the quality requirement for the test (e.g., 10% for cholesterol).
2. Scale the y-axis of the chart from 0 to TE_a (10% for cholesterol) and scale the x-axis from 0 to 0.5 TE_a (5.0% for cholesterol).
3. Label the y-axis "Observed inaccuracy (bias, %)" and label the x-axis "Observed imprecision (CV, %)".
4. Draw lines for the different goals for 2, 3, 4, 5, and 6 Sigma performance. The y-intercept of each line is TE_a; the x-intercept is TE_a/Sigma goal. For our cholesterol example,
   a. 2 Sigma line has a y-intercept is 10% (TE_a) and the x-intercept is 5% ($TE_a/2$);
   b. 3 Sigma line has a y-intercept of 10% and an x-intercept of 3.3% ($TE_a/3$);
   c. 4 Sigma line has a y-intercept of 10% and an x-intercept of 2.5% ($TE_a/4$);
   d. 5 Sigma line has a y-intercept of 10% and an x-intercept of 2.0% ($TE_a/5$);
   e. 6 Sigma line, y-intercept of 10% and x-intercept of 1.7% ($TE_a/6$).

5. Label the regions above the 2 Sigma line "unacceptable"; between the 2 and 3 Sigma lines "poor"; between the 4 Sigma and 3 Sigma lines "marginal;" between the 5 Sigma and 4 Sigma lines "good"; between the 6 Sigma and 5 Sigma lines "excellent"; and below the 6 Sigma line "world class."

6. To assess the analytical performance of a method, plot an "operating point" whose y-coordinate represents the observed bias and x-coordinate represents the observed imprecision.

The example points – A, B, and C – represent the example cholesterol methods for which the Sigma calculations (performed earlier in this chapter) gave results of 2.33 Sigma, 3.33 Sigma, and 5.0 Sigma.

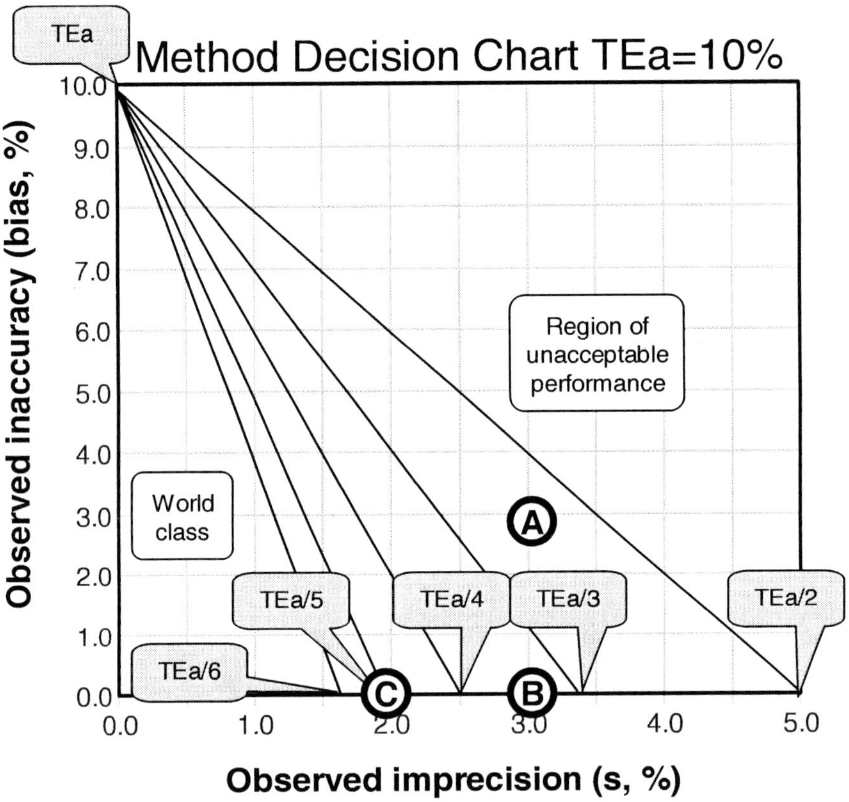

DOs and DON'Ts

- DO define the quality required for a test if you want to make an objective assessment of method performance.
- DO utilize the allowable total error format for defining an analytical quality requirement.
- DO start with the CLIA minimum requirements for acceptable analytical performance. Some people think these criteria are too loose, but they turn out to be quite demanding when the aim is to achieve 6 Sigma performance.
- DO calculate the Sigma metric for method performance to provide a quantitative description of performance relative to the goal for quality.
- DON'T worry too much about the estimate of bias when you're getting started. If necessary, assume bias is zero. That condition will give an optimistic estimate of the Sigma performance. If that performance is bad, you know you've got a problem. If that performance is good, then you can refine the estimate once you get better data.

References

1. Westgard JO. Six Sigma Quality Design and Control: Desirable precision and requisite QC for laboratory measurement processes. Madison WI:Westgard QC, Inc., 2001.
2. Nevalainen D, Berte L, Kraft C, Leigh E, Morgan T. Evaluating laboratory performance on quality indicates with the six sigma scale. Arch Pathol Lab Med 2000;124:516-519.
3. Ricos C, Alvarez V, Cava F. Current databases on biological variation: pros, cons and progress. Scand J Clin Lab Invest 1999;59:491-500.
4. Fraser CG. Biological Variation: From principles to practice. Washington DC:AACC Press, 2001.
5. Westgard JO, Carey RN, Wold S. Criteria for judging precision and accuracy in method development and evaluation. Clin Chem 1974;20:825-833.
6. Ehrmeyer SS, Laessig RH, Leinweber JE, Oryall JE. 1990 Medicare/CLIA final rules for proficiency testing: Minimum interlaboratory performance characteristics (CV and Bias) needed to pass. Clin Chem 1990;36:1736-1740.
7. Westgard JO, Burnett RW. Precision requirements for cost-effective operation of analytical processes. Clin Chem 1990;36:1629-1632.
8. Westgard JO. Basic Method Validation, 2nd edition. Madison WI:Westgard QC, Inc., 2003, chapter 16.

11: Final Quality Control Regulations

Unlike the method validation requirements, which were not in force until the Final Rule [1], CLIA has always had QC requirements for all non-waived laboratory tests since the first version of the CLIA Rules [2]. The implementation of these QC regulations has typically been carried out by CMS and COLA for small laboratories and CAP and JCAHO for large laboratories, though some healthcare organizations prefer to place their Near Patient Testing and Point of Care laboratories under JCAHO rather than CAP.

- CMS, The Centers for Medicare and Medicaid Services, formerly known as the Health Care Financing Administration (HCFA), will inspect any size laboratory, including physician office laboratories, for adherence to the CLIA standards;
- COLA, formerly known at the Commission of Office Laboratory Accreditation, inspects physician's office laboratories and small hospitals for adherence to COLA standards which closely parallel the CLIA regulations;
- JCAHO, The Joint Commission on Accreditation of Healthcare Organizations, inspects laboratories as part of an overall inspection of a hospital or healthcare organization;
- LAP-CAP, The Laboratory Accreditation Program of the College of American Pathologists, mainly inspects large laboratories directed by pathologists; CAP standards tend to be somewhat more stringent than the CLIA requirements to reflect the responsibilities expected of laboratory professionals.

The CLIA regulations for QC are based on test complexity, which is a measure of the difficulty to perform the test methodology. For purposes of QC, there are three categories of test complexity: waived, non-waived, and Provider-Performed Microscopy (PPM), which is reserved for a selected group of practitioners. Current information on test complexity can be obtained from the CLIA program's website [3].

QC and Test Complexity

Waived Tests. The list of waived tests continues to expand and now includes methodologies for more than 60 analytes. That's part of the reason for eliminating the distinction between moderate and high complexity tests (now lumped together as non-waived) in the Final Rule – many moderate complexity tests are now classified as waived tests. Subpart K, Quality Systems for Nonwaived Testing, begins with these general requirements:

§493.1200 (a) Each laboratory that performs nonwaived testing must establish and maintain written policies and procedures that implement and monitor quality systems for all phases of the total testing process (that is, preanalytic, analytic, and postanalytic), as well as general laboratory systems. (b) The laboratory's quality systems must include a quality assessment component that ensures continuous improvement of the laboratory's performance and services through ongoing monitoring that identifies, evaluates and resolves problems. (c) The various components of the laboratory's quality system are used to meet the requirements in this part and must be appropriate for the specialties and subspecialties of testing the laboratory performs, services it offers, and clients it serves.

- Under CLIA and COLA [4], the minimum requirement for anyone performing waived testing is to follow the manufacturer's directions including recommendations or suggestions for QC. If the manufacturer identifies no specific QC requirements, then testing sites are expected to follow good laboratory practices, which usually dictate that controls be run and results documented and reviewed for correctness before reporting patient results.

Provider Performed Microscopy (PPM). In January 1993, CMS established "Physician-Performed Microscopy," a subset of the moderate complexity test category. In 1995 it was renamed "Provider-Performed Microscopy." This category is exclusively for physicians, dentists, nurse practitioners and midwives, and physician assistants who perform these tests as part of a patient examination. The primary instrument for performing PPM tests is the microscope.

The PPM tests identified below as well as all the waived tests can be performed under a PPM CLIA certificate. The practitioners are expected to follow the manufacturer's directions for QC and follow good laboratory practices. The PPM category includes all direct wet mount preparations (suspended in saline or water) for the presence or absence of bacteria, fungi, parasites and human cellular elements, KOH preps, pinworm exams, fern tests, post-coital direct qualitative exams of vaginal or cervical mucous, urine sediment exams, nasal smears for granulocytes, fecal leukocyte exams, and qualitative semen analysis (limited to the presence or absence of sperm and detection of motility).

Nonwaived Tests. The January 2003 Final CLIA Rule [1] updated the QC requirements in the new Subpart K (Quality Systems for Nonwaived Testing). QC for nonwaived testing replaces the former and differing QC requirements for the moderate and high complexity test categories with a single set of requirements for both, as shown below:

§493.1256 Standard: Control procedures.

(a) For each test system, the laboratory is responsible for having control procedures that monitor the accuracy and precision of the complete analytic process.

(b) The laboratory must establish the number, type, and frequency of testing control materials using, if applicable, the performance specifications verified or established by the laboratory as specified in §493.1253(b)(3).

(c) The control procedure must (1) detect immediate errors that occur due to test system failure, adverse environmental conditions, and operator performance. (2) Monitor over time the accuracy and precision of test performance that may be influenced by changes in test system performance and environmental conditions, and variance in operator performance.

(d) Unless CMS approves a procedure, specified in Appendix C of the State Operations Manual (CMS Pub. 7), that provides equivalent quality testing, the laboratory must

(1) perform control procedures as defined in this section unless otherwise specified in the additional specialty and subspecialty requirements at §493.1261 through 493.1278.

(2) For each test system, perform control procedures using the number and frequency specified by the manufacturer or established by the laboratory when they meet or exceed the requirements in paragraph (d)(3) of this section.

(3) At least once each day patient specimens are assayed or examined perform the following for-

(i) Each quantitative procedure, include two control materials of different concentrations;

(ii) Each qualitative procedure, include a negative and positive control material;

(iii) Test procedures producing graded or titered results, include a negative control material and a control material with graded or titered reactivity, respectively;

(iv) Each test system that has an extraction phase, include two control materials, including one that is capable of detecting errors in the extraction process; and

(v) Each molecular amplification procedure, include two control materials and, if reaction inhibition is a significant source of false negative results, a control material capable of detecting the inhibition.

(4) For thin layer chromatography—

(i) Spot each plate or card, as applicable, with a calibrator containing all known substances or drug groups, as appropriate, which are identified by thin layer chromatography and reported by the laboratory; and

(ii) Include at least one control material on each plate or card, as applicable, which must be processed through each step of patient testing, including extraction processes.

(5) For each electrophoretic procedure include, concurrent with patient specimens, at least one control material containing the substances being identified or measured.

(6) Perform control material testing as specified in this paragraph before resuming patient testing when a complete change of reagents is introduced; major preventive maintenance is performed; or any critical part that may influence test performance is replaced.

(7) Over time, rotate control material testing among all operators who perform the test.

(8) Test control materials in the same manner as patient specimens.

(9) When using calibration material as a control material, use calibration material from a different lot number than that used to establish a cut-off value or to calibrate the test system.

(10) Establish or verify the criteria for acceptability of all control materials.

(i) When control materials providing quantitative results are used, statistical parameters (for example, mean and standard deviation) for each batch and lot number of control materials must be defined and available.

(ii) The laboratory may use the stated value of a commercially assayed control material provided the stated value is for the methodology and instrumentation employed by the laboratory and is verified by the laboratory.

(iii) Statistical parameters for unassayed control materials must be established over time by the laboratory through concurrent testing of control materials having previously determined statistical parameters.

(e) For reagent, media, and supply checks, the laboratory must do the following:

(1) Check each batch (prepared in-house), lot number (commercially prepared) and shipment of reagents, disks,

stains, antisera, and identification systems (systems using two or more substrates or two or more reagents, or a combination) when prepared or opened for positive and negative reactivity, as well as graded reactivity, if applicable.

(2) Each day of use (unless otherwise specified in this subpart), test staining materials for intended reactivity to ensure predictable staining characteristics. Control materials for both positive and negative reactivity must be included, as appropriate.

(3) Check fluorescent and immunohistochemical stains for positive and negative reactivity each time of use.

(4) Before, or concurrent with the initial use—

(i) Check each batch of media for sterility if sterility is required for testing;

(ii) Check each batch of media for its ability to support growth and, as appropriate, select or inhibit specific organisms or produce a biochemical response; and

(iii) Document the physical characteristics of the media when compromised and report any deterioration in the media to the manufacturer.

(5) Follow the manufacturer's specifications for using reagents, media, and supplies and be responsible for results.

(f) Results of control materials must meet the laboratory's and, as applicable, the manufacturer's test system criteria for acceptability before reporting patient test results.

(g) The laboratory must document all control procedures performed.

(h) If control materials are not available, the laboratory must have an alternative mechanism to detect immediate errors and monitor test system performance over time. The performance of alternative control procedures must be documented.

Specialty control procedures are given in sections §493.1261 - §493.1278 for bacteriology, mycobacteriology (.1261), mycology (.1262), parasitology (.1263), virology (.1264), routine chemistry

(.1267), hematology (.1269), immunohematology (.1271), histopathology (.1273), cytology (.1274), clinical cytogenetics (.1276), and histocompatability (.1278). For common chemistry and hematology tests, the additional details are as follows:

§493.1267 Standard: Routine chemistry.

For blood gas analyses, the laboratory must perform the following:

(a) Calibrate or verify calibration according to the manufacturer's specifications and with at least the frequency recommended by the manufacturer.

(b) Test one sample of control material each 8 hours of testing using a combination of control materials that include both low and high values on each day of testing.

(c) Test one sample of control material each time specimens are tested unless automated instrumentation internally verifies calibration at least every 30 minutes.

(d) Document all control procedures performed, as specified in this section.

§493.1269 Standard: Hematology.

(a) For manual cell counts performed using a hemocytometer—

(1) One control material must be tested each 8 hours of operation; and

(2) Patient specimens and control materials must be tested in duplicate.

(b) For all nonmanual coagulation test systems, the laboratory must include two levels of control material each 8 hours of operation and each time a reagent is changed.

(c) For manual coagulation tests—

(1) Each individual performing tests must test two levels of control materials before testing patient samples and each time a reagent is changed; and

(2) Patient specimens and control materials must be tested in duplicate.

(d) The laboratory must document all control procedures performed, as specified in this section.

For those methodologies where the manufacturer specifies surrogate or electronic controls or process controls to fulfill the daily QC requirement, make sure to read carefully §493.1256 (d) where the new QC concept – equivalent quality testing – is introduced. Appendix C, Regulations and Interpretive Guidelines for Laboratories and Laboratory Services, of the State Operations Manual (SOM) provide more information [5]. "Equivalent QC procedures" (Eqc) are discussed in detail in Chapter 14.

In all cases, documentation of both the QC results and the specific remedial action to "out of control results" (Section §493.1282 – Corrective Actions) must be followed and the policies and procedures along with the specific actions must be available to the inspector.

JCAHO Requirements for Quality Monitoring and Control Systems

The requirements identified for CMS (CLIA) also are applicable to JCAHO. Under JCAHO, the goal of QC is to achieve quality in laboratory testing and produce the best possible test results and outcomes.

Waived Tests. JCAHO recognizes waived tests (WT) as defined by CLIA, but identifies additional quality and QC requirements that include [6]:

- *(WT.1.10) Definition of the extent of use of the waived test,(i.e., definitively or only as a screen);*
- *(WT.1.20) Identification of testing personnel and supervisory staff responsible for testing activities;*
- *(WT.1.30) Documentation that staff performing tests have adequate, specific training and orientation to perform the tests and maintain satisfactory levels of competence;*
- *(WT.1.40) Proof that all testing personnel have access to current written policies and procedures governing specific testing-related activities;*

- *(WT.1.50) Defined (by the laboratory) QC checks that at least meet the minimum manufacturer's recommendations are conducted on each procedure (two levels of QC are required for each automated procedure each day of testing);*
- *(WT.1.60) Maintenance of appropriate QC and test records.*

Nonwaived Tests. General Quality Monitoring and Control System Requirements (Each specialty area has additional requirements):

- *(QC.1.10) Each specialty and subspecialty (of testing) has a documented QC program.*
- *(QC.1.70) The laboratory's QC system includes the validation of methods used.*
- *(QC.1.80) The laboratory evaluates and correlates the relationship between results for the same test performed with different methods or instruments or at different sites.*
- *(QC.1.90) The testing sites QC system includes daily and periodic surveillance of results by appropriate personnel.*
- *(QC.1.100) The testing site takes remedial action for deficiencies identified through QC measures or authorized inspections and documents such actions.*
- *(QC.1.110) The site ensures that QC results meet its criteria for acceptability before it reports patient test results.*
- *(QC.1.120) QC specimens are tested in the same manner as patient samples*
- *(QC.1.130) The laboratory follows written guidelines for the proper preparation, storage, dispensing, and periodic evaluation of all reagents, including water, to provide for accuracy and precision of results.*
- *(QC.1.140) The laboratory ensures that reagents and solutions are completely and accurately labeled according to written guidelines.*
- *(QC.1.150) The laboratory retains QC records as required by law.*

Clinical Chemistry QC Requirements:

- *(QC.6.10) Using appropriate controls, the laboratory verifies each procedure in clinical chemistry at least once each day of use.*

- *(QC.6.20) The laboratory maintains and evaluates data on the routine precision of test results and performs calibration verification and recalibration as required.*
- *(QC.6.30) The laboratory establishes its own control ranges with valid statistical measurements for each procedure in chemistry.*
- *(QC.6.40) The laboratory establishes and makes available to its staff acceptable limits for all standard and reference QC samples as well as the action to take when results are outside satisfactory control limits.*
- *(QC.6.50) The laboratory established test control limits and reportable ranges to provide results with meaningful clinical applications.*

Hematology and Coagulation QC Requirements:

- *(QC.7.10) The laboratory verifies each procedure and test parameter against known standards or controls within the range of clinically significant values each day of use.*
- *(QC.7.20) Using repetitive testing, the laboratory establishes control ranges with valid statistical measurements for each procedure in hematology and coagulation.*
- *(QC.7.30) The laboratory has established and makes available to its staff acceptable limits for all standard and reference QC samples as well as the action to take when results are outside satisfactory control limits.*
- *(QC.7.40) The laboratory establishes test control limits and reportable ranges to provide results with meaningful clinical applications.*
- *(QC.7.50) The laboratory takes appropriate measures to provide reliable results when performing blood cell counts using manual methods.*
- *(QC.7.60) Reliable tests for detecting hemostatic and coagulation defects are available.*
- *(QC.7.70) The laboratory ensures that manual coagulation tests are accurate.*

CAP Laboratory Accreditation Program Requirements for Quality Control

CAP's philosophy is that all clinical laboratory tests, regardless of the CMS test complexity classification, need to follow essentially the same quality requirements. All test specialty areas must follow the quality requirements identified in the Laboratory General Checklist (GEN) as well as those identified in the checklist for the particular area of testing, e.g., the Point-of-Care Testing Checklist (POC). For all testing, LAP-CAP requires an audit trail that ties the patients' results with the analyst, instrument and QC. In addition, there must be at least monthly review of QC data by the director or director's designee.

For the general requirements, CAP states in the Laboratory General Checklist (GEN, July 2003) [7] that the *overall quality control program for the entire laboratory must be clearly defined and documented. It must include general policies and delegation of responsibilities. The quality control records should be well organized with a defined system to permit regular review by appropriate supervisory personnel (laboratory director, supervisor or laboratory quality control coordinator).*

- *(GEN.30000) Is there a written QC program that clearly defines procedures for monitoring analytic performance, including establishment of tolerance limits, number and frequency of controls, corrective actions based on QC data, and related information?*
- *(GEN.30050) For those tests performed using different methodologies or instruments or at different testing sites, is there a documented mechanism to verify the comparability of patient results throughout the clinically appropriate ranges?* Note that CAP considers identical makes and models of a particular instrument as separate systems.
- *(GEN.30070) If the laboratory performs test procedures for which neither calibration nor control materials are available, have procedures been established to verify the reliability of patient test results?*
- *(GEN.30200) Are quality control records retained for at least 2 years?*

- *(GEN.30300) Has the laboratory conducted an interim self inspection and documented efforts to correct deficiencies identified during that process?*

Examples of QC requirements from additional discipline checklists — POC (Point-of-Care Testing – December 2003), LSV (Limited Service Laboratory – December 2003), CHM (Chemistry and Toxicology – December 2003), and HEM (Hematology and Coagulation, July 2003) — follow:

- *(POC.03500, LSV.00500, CHM.10500, HEM.20000) Does the laboratory have a written QC/QI program to ensure quality throughout the pre-analytical, analytical and post-analytical phases of testing?*
- *(POC. 06450, LSV.00700, CHM.10700, HEM.20150) Is there evidence of ongoing evaluation of records of controls, instrument maintenance and function checks, temperature, etc., for all procedures on all shifts?*
- *(POC.03700, LSV.01100 - .01400, CHM.10800, HEM.20150) Is there a documented system to detect and correct significant clerical and analytical errors, and unusual/unexpected test results?*
- *(POC.08900, LSV.40850, CHM.14000) For quantitative tests, has a statistically valid acceptable range been established for each lot of control material by repetitive analysis in runs that include previously tested control materials?*
- *(POC.05900, LSV.41010, CHM.14300) Are QC data organized and presented so they can be evaluated daily by the technical staff to detect problems, trends, etc.?*
- *(POC.06200, LSV.41170, CHM.14600, HEM.34150) Is there evidence of corrective action when control results exceed defined tolerance limits?*
- *(POC.09000, LSV.41130, CHM.14500, HEM.20050) For numeric QC data, are QC statistics (e.g., SD or CV) calculated at specified intervals to define analytic imprecision?*

Issues and Answers

Are there any substantial differences in the QC requirements for all of the inspection and accreditation organizations?

The QC requirements are pretty much the same – they have to be since all organizations must be approved by CMS to conduct laboratory inspections used to satisfy government regulatory requirements. However, there might be some differences in the agendas of different accreditation organizations and therefore a difference in emphasis, or attention to certain issues, when they inspect a laboratory. COLA and CMS are expected to be more supportive of practices in small laboratories. CAP is expected to have more rigorous standards of practice for large laboratories and also will impose those practices on POC operations. JCAHO falls somewhere in between, being more lenient than CAP on POC laboratories but having more stringent requirements for organization-wide quality improvement activities. Even if a laboratory chooses CAP inspection, JCAHO will audit the laboratory's role in organization-wide quality initiatives.

Are there any other "standards" that provide guidance for QC?

NCCLS is another source of standards and guidelines for laboratory practice and provides two documents that deal with laboratory QC practices.

- C24-A2 [8] provides guidelines for statistical QC, including the definition of an analytical run, steps for planning or selecting a QC procedure, desirable characteristics of control materials, and recommended practices for routine operation of a QC procedure, including frequency and location of control samples, decision criteria or control rules, calculation of control limits on the basis of cumulative means and SDs, and what to do in out-of-control situations.

- EP18-A [9] provides guidelines for developing a quality system for unit-use devices. It focuses more on individual methods for monitoring specific sources of errors and attempts to avoid the use of statistical QC because of the difficulties of implementation in Near Patient Testing or Point-of-Care applications. CLIA cites EP18-A in its recommendations for "equivalent QC procedures," which are aimed primarily at Physician Office Labs and NPT/POC applications where CLIA has not yet been successful in achieving compliance with their minimum QC standards.

ISO (International Standards Organization) that publishes guidelines for quality management that are used in many industries, including healthcare laboratories.

- ISO/FDIS 15189 [10] is a new document that provides guidelines specifically for medical laboratories. Its requirement for QC is found in paragraph 5.6.1, which reads "The laboratory shall design internal quality control systems that verify the attainment of the intended quality of results." While the intention is clear, there is no detailed information on how to accomplish this. ISO assumes a highly competent professional will know what to do and will be responsible for implementation and operation of effective QC procedures. Contrast that with CLIA, where CMS aims for the lowest standard that can be implemented by non-technical people who have minimal training and competence.

DOs and DON'Ts

- DO follow the manufacturer's QC instructions. You can always do more, but you can't do less.
- DO recognize that the CLIA requirement for immediate error detection and CLIA minimum standard of running 2 controls per 24 hours are not consistent. You should run controls more frequently to detect immediate errors. You should do this whenever there are changes in the testing process, whenever you are suspicious that something may be going wrong, whenever there is any question about the quality of the test results.

- DO remember that good laboratory practice and professional responsibility are as important, actually more important, than the minimum CLIA requirements.
- DON'T forget about the specialty QC requirements that follow the general requirements. You need to read them carefully because they contain specific requirements that apply to specific areas of testing.
- DON'T assume that the laboratory should use 2 SD control limits. There is no recommendation for that practice anywhere in the regulations or interpretive guidelines. And that practice causes a high level of false rejections, which compromises the laboratory's ability to detect and fix real problems. See Chapter 12 for guidance on doing QC right.
- DON'T reduce your QC to CLIA minimums just because you can get by doing less. Remember that CLIA is aimed at laboratories that have no history of doing QC and is attempting to get them to do *some* QC. Large laboratories should not reduce their QC to the CLIA minimums without careful assessment that those minimums are adequate for patient care. See Chapter 13 for guidance on doing the right QC.
- DON'T adopt "equivalent QC procedures" without careful study and evaluation. See Chapters 14 and 15 for more guidance.

References

1. US Centers for Medicare & Medicaid Services (CMS). Medicare, Medicaid, and CLIA Programs: Laboratory Requirements Relating to quality Systems and Certain Personnel Qualifications. Final Rule. Fed Regist Jan 24 2003;16:3640-3714. http://www.phppo.cdc.gov/clia/regs/toc.aspx

2. U.S. Department of Health and Human Services. Medicare, Medicaid and CLIA programs: Regulations implementing the Clinical Laboratory Improvement Amendments of 1988 (CLIA). Final rule. Fed Regist 1992; 57:7002-186.

3. http://www.cms.hhs.gov/clia/default.asp CLIA Program Clinical Laboratory Improvement Amendments.

4. Accreditation Manual. COLA. Columbia, MD, 2004.

5. CMS State Operations Manual Appendix C, Regulations and Interpretive Guidelines for Laboratories and Laboratory Services, http://www.cms.gov/clia/appendc.asp

6. 2004 Comprehensive Accreditation Manual for Laboratory and Point-of-Care. Joint Commission on Accreditation of Healthcare Organizations (JCAHO). Oakbrook Terrace, IL, 2003.

7. Checklists. Laboratory Accreditation Program. College of American Pathologists (CAP). Northfield, IL, 2003. Available at http://www.cap.org

8. NCCLS C24-A2. Statistical quality control for quantitative measurements: Principles and definitions; Approved guideline - Second edition. National Committee for Clinical Laboratory Standards, 940 West Valley Road, Wayne, PA 19087, USA, 1999.

9. NCCLS EP-18A. Quality management for unit-use testing; Approved guideline. National Committee for Clinical Laboratory Standards, 940 West Valley Road, Wayne, PA 19087 USA, 2002.

10. ISO/FDIS 15189. Medical laboratories – Particular requirements for quality and competence. International Standards Organization, Geneva, Switzerland, 2002.

Online References

JCAHO: http://www.jcaho.org

CAP: http://www.cap.org

COLA: http://www.cola.org

CLIA information (waived tests, test complexities, federal registers, etc.)

CMS: http://www.cms.hhs.gov/clia/default.asp

CDC: http://www.phppo.cdc.gov/clia/default.asp

12: Doing QC Right

This chapter provides an overview of the process of establishing and operating a statistical QC procedure. The objective is to review all the activities that are necessary to perform QC properly. More detailed information is available at the Internet links that will be referenced. An expanded and updated version is available in hardcopy, in the *Basic QC Practices* manual [1].

The purpose of QC is to help people do good work by giving them a way to check that their work processes are functioning properly. People need tools, such as statistical QC, to help them do this. Statistical QC provides a way of looking at the results of a work process and identifying when they exceed the variation expected under stable routine operation, in which case, it is likely that something has gone wrong and that the process needs to be fixed.

Statistical QC is advantageous because it provides a single universally applicable technique for monitoring the complete analytic process, including test system components, environmental factors, and operator skills. In spite of the long history of using statistical QC in laboratories, it is still fraught with problems due to the lack of understanding of the principles and best practices. These problems are exacerbated in Point-of-Care applications where there is minimal operator training and experience. Similar problems are also being seen in clinical laboratories, where the shortage of trained clinical laboratory scientists, technologists, and technicians has led to lowered skills and less experience.

The CLIA Rules

§493.1256 Standard: Control procedures. [2]

(a) For each test system, the laboratory is responsible for having control procedures that monitor the accuracy and precision of the complete analytic process.

(b) The laboratory must establish the number, type, and frequency of testing control materials using, if applicable, the performance specifications verified or established by the laboratory as specified in §493.1253(b)(3).

(c) The control procedure must (1) detect immediate errors that occur due to test system failure, adverse environmental conditions, and operator performance. (2) Monitor over time the accuracy and precision of test performance that may be influenced by changes in test system performance and environmental conditions, and variance in operator performance.

(d) Unless CMS approves a procedure, specified in Appendix C of the State Operations Manual (CMS Pub. 7), that provides equivalent quality testing, the laboratory must (1) perform control procedures as defined in this section unless otherwise specified in the additional specialty and subspecialty requirements at §493.1261 through 493.1278. (2) For each test system, perform control procedures using the number and frequency specified by the manufacturer or established by the laboratory when they meet or exceed the requirements in paragraph (d)(3) of this section.

D5441

Interpretive Guidelines 493.1256(C) CONTROL PROCEDURES
[3] In determining the control procedures, including the frequency of testing controls that detect immediate errors and monitor test performance over time, the laboratory needs to consider the following:

- *Control procedures specified by the test system's manufacturer;*
- *Test system instrument and reagent stability (e.g., relocation);*
- *Frequency and volume of test performance;*
- *Technique dependence of the method;*
- *Frequency of quality control failures;*
- *Training, experience, and competency of technical personnel.*

Traditionally, laboratories have tested two levels of external control materials daily to monitor the accuracy and precision of the analytic test system components. External control materials have a similar matrix to that of patient specimens, are treated in the same manner as patient specimens, and go through all analytic phases of testing. External control materials may be provided as part of the test system, provided separately or prepared in-house. Testing external controls meets the requirement for monitoring test system components, environment, and operator performance. External control materials may be:

- *Commercially or in-house prepared controls;*
- *Proficiency testing specimens for which results have been confirmed;*
- *Reference or control strains of microorganisms;*
- *Calibrators of different lot numbers and concentration than those used to calibrate the system; or*
- *Previously tested patient specimens provided the laboratory determines the acceptable performance level for the patient specimens.*

Definitions of Terms

The definitions given here can be found in the *Basic QC Practices* manual [1]. These terms are expected to be commonly understood by laboratory personnel, but it is important to that there is a shared understanding of their meaning.

- **QC procedure, control procedure.** The protocol and materials that are necessary for an analyst to test whether the method is working properly and patient test results can be reported. A QC procedure can be described by the number of control measurements and the decision criteria (control rules) used for judging the acceptability of analytical results.
- **Control material.** A control sample or solution that is available, often commercially, liquid or lyophilized, and packaged in aliquots that can be prepared and used individually to provide ongoing testing on a uniform and stable specimen.
- **External control material.** The modifier "external" means that this material is outside the analytical system and is

sampled like an individual patient specimen. The SOM makes specific mention of external control materials, even though this term doesn't appear in the Final CLIA regulations.

- **Control measurement.** The analytical result that is obtained when a control material is analyzed.

- **Number of control measurements.** Generally refers to the number of control results that are available for inspection when assessing the control status of the analytical testing process. CLIA generally requires 2 control measurements during a 24 hour period. For certain tests, the requirement is 1 control measurement during an 8 hour period or workshift, which could mean as many as 3 during a 24 hour period.

- **Analytical run.** Generally defined by CLIA as an 8 hour to 24 hour interval during which control materials must be analyzed. The NCCLS C24-A2 document [4] defines a run as "an interval (i.e., a period of time or series of measurements) within which the accuracy and precision of the measuring system is expected to be stable. In laboratory operations, control samples are analyzed during each analytical run to evaluate method performance, therefore the analytical run defines the interval (period of time or number of specimens) between evaluations of control results. Between quality control evaluations, events may occur causing the measurement process to be susceptible to variations that are important to detect."

- **Control status.** Refers to the outcome of the QC process and a decision that the analytical run is "in-control," in which case patient results can be reported, or "out-of-control," in which case the patient results should be held, the problem identified and resolved, and the patient samples analyzed again.

- **Control chart.** A graphical method for displaying control results and evaluating whether a testing process is in-control or out-of-control. Control results are plotted versus time or sequential run number to display the results relative to the expected mean and control limits drawn on the chart.

- **Control limits.** Lines drawn on a control chart to provide graphic criteria for assessing whether a measurement procedure is in-control or out-of-control. The control limits are usually calculated from the mean and standard deviation determined for a given control material. Typically control limits are drawn at the mean plus and minus 2 or 3 SDs. CAP uses the term "tolerance limits" in the General Checklist and "statistically valid acceptable range" in the Chemistry and Toxicology Checklist.

- **Control rule.** A decision criterion for judging whether an analytical run is in-control or out-of-control. It is commonly defined by a symbol of the form A_L, where A is an abbreviation for a statistic or represents a number of control measurements, and L identifies the control limits, often specified as the mean ± a multiple of the standard deviation (s). For example:

    - $\mathbf{1_{3s}}$ refers to a control rule used with a Levey-Jennings chart when the control limits are set as the mean +3s and the mean -3s. A run is considered out-of-control when a single control measurement exceeds either limit.

    - $\mathbf{1_{2s}}$ refers to a control rule where the control limits are set as the mean ± 2s. We recommend that 2s control limits be used only as a warning rule in multirule procedures ("Westgard Rules"), rather than as a rejection rule on its own.

    - $\mathbf{2_{2s}}$ refers to a control rule where a run is rejected when 2 consecutive measurements exceed the same mean +2s control limit or the same mean -2s control limit.

    - $\mathbf{R_{4s}}$ refers to a control rule where a run is rejected when 1 control measurement in the group exceeds the mean +2s control limit and another exceeds the mean -2s control limit.

    - $\mathbf{4_{1s}}$ refers to a control rule where a run is rejected when 4 consecutive control measurements exceed the same mean + 1s or the same mean -1s control limit.

- **10_x** refers to a control rule where a run is rejected when 10 consecutive control measurements fall on the same side of the mean.

- **Multirule QC.** Refers to the use of a combination of control rules for evaluation of the control results, e.g., the combination $1_{3s}/2_{2s}/R_{4s}/4_{1s}/10x$ is widely known and commonly referred to as the "Westgard Rules" [5].

Issues and Answers

How does statistical QC work?

The principle of statistical QC is to first determine the variation that can be expected from a stable process, then to monitor that variation to see if there are any changes that indicate the process has become unstable. The easiest way to monitor the process variation is to analyze a stable sample (control material) again and again. QC can be considered as an extension of the replication experiment that was initially performed to validate the precision of the method. In fact, that data can be used to calculate the mean and standard deviation (SD or s) that are used to set up a control chart. Ongoing measurements on the same material are then displayed over time to emphasize any changes that occur during the routine operation of the method, as shown in the accompanying figure.

Given that measurement variation typically shows a normal or Gaussian distribution of results, it can be expected that 68% of those results will be within ± 1 standard deviation (s or SD) of the mean, 95% within ± 2s of the mean and 99.7% within ± 3s of the mean. Control limits are drawn on the control chart to help identify results that are unexpected and need to be investigated. [See QC – The Idea: www.westgard.com/lesson11.htm]

How do you set up a QC procedure?

Statistical QC is a quantitative technique and must be properly implemented to work correctly and accomplish its intended purpose.

- Choose appropriate control materials. This includes the number of materials necessary to monitor the critical medical decision

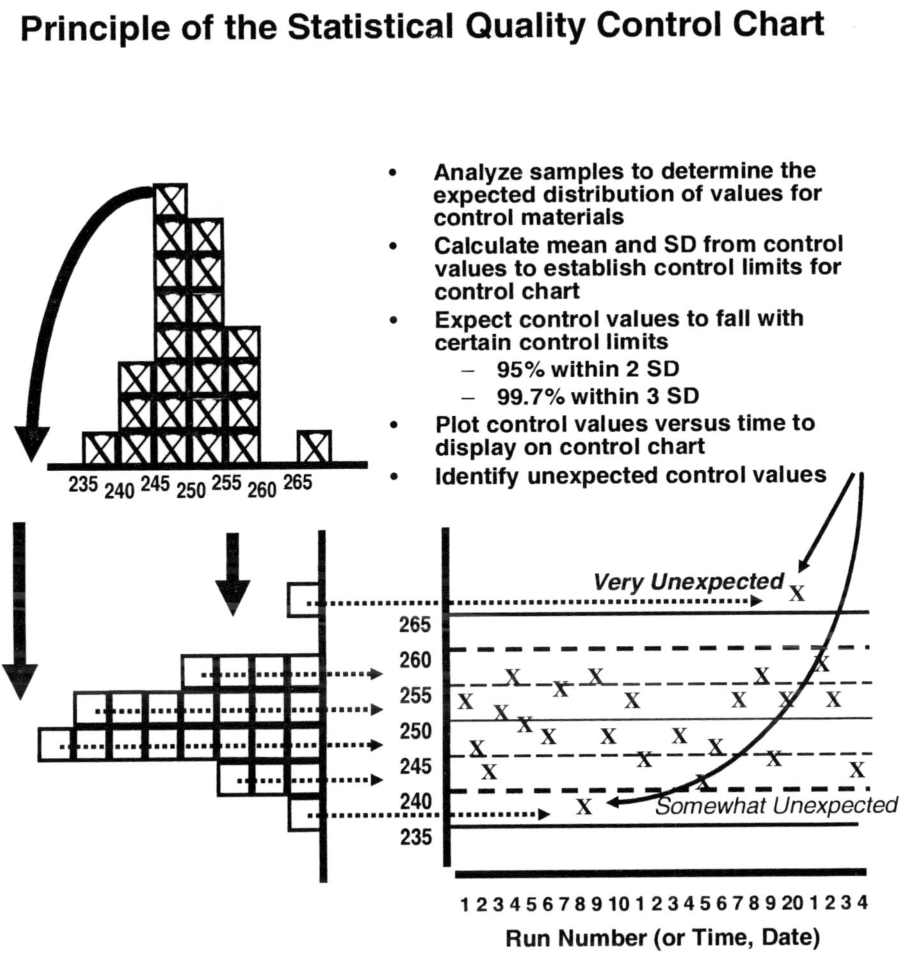

levels and working range of the method, as well as the type of material that will best simulate the true patient sample. It is common practice to use two levels of controls for many chemistry tests and three levels for hematology and coagulation tests. [See QC – The Materials: www.westgard.com/lesson13.htm]

- ❍ **D5447** provides some guidance on the selection of controls that have appropriate matrix and indicates they should monitor both normal and abnormal concentrations.

- Analyze the control materials to obtain a minimum of 20 measurements over at least a 10 day period. It is important to collect measurements that will characterize the actual performance of the method under each laboratory's own operating conditions. Ten days is a minimum period to observe factors that affect method performance; 20 days is better.

  - ❍ **D5469** recommends 20 replicate tests be performed to determine a standard deviation. There is no guideline on the time period.

  - ❍ **D5469** *Probes §493.1256(d)(10). What statistics does the laboratory have to demonstrate the number of assays and the period of time in which the laboratory repetitively tested control materials to verify or establish control limits?*

- Calculate the mean and standard deviation of the control measurements. While the number of measurements may be minimal in the beginning, the mean and standard deviation can be updated as more measurements are accumulated. [See QC – The Calculations: www.westgard.com/lesson14.htm]

- Calculate the control limits for the control rules that are to be applied. Contrary to some manufacturers' instructions and some laboratory practices, it is not advisable to use the bottle values appearing on control materials to set statistical control limits. Control limits should be calculated from the mean and standard deviation that were determined when that control material was analyzed in the laboratory.

  - ❍ CAP is very clear that the laboratory must establish a "statistically valid acceptable range" for each control material from data on repetitive analyses in the laboratory [CHM.14000].

  - ❍ Note below, however, that CLIA allows use of the manufacturer's stated values if the laboratory verifies them.

- ❍ **§493.1256 (d)(10) Establish or verify the criteria for acceptability of all control materials.**
- ❍ **(d)(10)(i) When control materials providing quantitative results are used, statistical parameters (for example, mean and standard deviation) for each batch and lot number of control materials must be defined and available.**
- ❍ **(d)(10)(ii) The laboratory may use the stated value of a commercially assayed control material provided the stated value is for the methodology and instrumentation employed by the laboratory and is verified by the laboratory.**
- ❍ **(d)(10)(iii) Statistical parameters for unassayed control materials must be established over time by the laboratory through concurrent testing of control materials having previously determined statistical parameters.**
- ❍ **D5469** *Interpretive Guidelines 493.1256(d)(10). Acceptable ranges must be verified (assayed) or established (unassayed) by the laboratory for control materials and any calibrators that are used in lieu of control materials. If laboratories rely on commercial companies to establish statistical limits for controls, the laboratory must have documentation to verify that its control results correlate with the established limits.*

- Prepare control charts or set the appropriate parameters in a computerized monitoring and charting package. A sheet of graph paper is all that's needed for manual implementation, however, computerized implementation is often necessary for high speed multitest automated analyzers that produce many control results in a short period of time. This computer support may be provided by software in the analyzer, by a PC data management station, or by a laboratory information system. [See QC – The Levey Jennings Control Chart: www.westgard.com/lesson12.htm.]

- Prepare written guidelines to document the operation of the QC procedure. Written protocols are required by accreditation and regulatory agencies, as well as for good laboratory practice. An important part of this protocol is to describe when control samples are to be analyzed, how many samples are to be analyzed, where they are to be located in an analytical run, how the control results are to be interpreted, and what to do when "out-of-control."
    - ❍ **D5469** *Probes §493.1256(d)(10. How does the laboratory evaluate control results to detect any outliers, shifts or trends in control values due to instrument malfunctions or changes in the analytical system?*
- Teach the QC procedure to ALL personnel who will be performing the test.

How does QC operate on a routine basis?

Routine operation depends on obtaining current control results and using them to determine whether the testing process is performing as expected. It is "expected" that the current control results fall within the established control limits if the testing process is working correctly. It is unexpected for the control results to exceed a control limit or violate a control rule – unless there is a problem with the testing process.

- Analyze control materials with each analytical run. Note that the run is defined by the written QC guidelines that were developed above. A run is typically defined in terms of a length of time, a number of samples analyzed, or a physical grouping (or batch) of samples. The definition of a run is subjective and may change as experience is gained and more information becomes available about a method's stability or frequency of problems.
    - ❍ §493.1256(d)(5) specifies that controls must be tested whenever there is a complete change of reagents, major preventive maintenance, or replacement of any critical part that may influence test performance.

- §493.1256(d)(7) specifies that the testing of controls should be rotated among all operators who perform the test.

- §493.1256(d)(8) specifies that control materials must be tested in the same manner as patient materials.

- Record the control results and plot on control charts (as necessary). According to the government, if you didn't write it down, you didn't do it. More importantly, the records are a critical source of information about the actual performance of the method under the real operating conditions of a laboratory.

  - **§493.1256(g) The laboratory must document all control procedures performed.**

  - **D5481** *Interpretive Guidelines. The actual measurement(s) taken, reactions and/or observations must be recorded.*

- Review and interpret the control results to determine control status. Here's where the decision criteria or control rules are important for achieving uniform interpretation regardless of the experience of the person performing the test. [See QC – The "Westgard Rules": www.westgard.com/mltirule.htm.]

- When control results are "in-control," i.e., none of the control rules are violated, accept the run and report the patient test results. Our philosophy is that each analyst should have sufficient training and experience to do this on their own, however, there may be situations where supervisory review is necessary before patient test results can be released. [See QC – The Multirule Interpretation: www.westgard.com/lesson18.htm.]

- When control results are "out-of-control," i.e., one of the control rules is violated, reject the run and do not report patient test results. Inspect the process, identify the source of difficulty, correct the problem, then re-analyze the patients and controls. Note that the particular control rule that is violated may be helpful in trouble-shooting; the 1_{3s} and R_{4s} rules tend to be more sensitive to random errors, whereas rules such as 2_{2s}

and $2of3_{2s}$ tend to be more sensitive to systematic errors. Random and systematic errors have different causes, thus the problem can be narrowed down to fewer possible sources. Once a problem is fixed, it may be best to re-analyze the controls first to determine control status, then re-assay the patient samples. [See QC – The Out-of-control Problem: www.westgard.com/lesson17.htm.]

❍ **§493.1256(f) Results of control materials must meet the laboratory's and, as applicable, the manufacturer's test system criteria for acceptability before reporting patient test results.**

- Document all control results, any control problems, and whatever was done to solve them. For unusual problems, it may be useful to file a detailed trouble-shooting report for future reference and use in training new personnel.

What documentation and review is necessary?

Because many factors are involved in maintaining quality, a system of records and documentation is needed for periodic review and evaluation.

- Maintain QC records for an appropriate period of time to document routine maintenance, unscheduled maintenance, reagent lot numbers in use and expiration dates, calibration records that include calibrator lot numbers and expiration dates, control results and summary statistics (monthly means and standard deviations, as well as cumulative means, standard deviations, and control limits in use), QC problems and corrective actions taken, and trouble-shooting reports. Most records need to be kept for two years according to US regulations, except that maintenance records must be kept for the lifetime of an instrument system and transferred with the instrument. [See QC – The Records: www.westgard.com/lesson19.htm.]

- Review monthly means for trends and small shifts that indicate systematic errors or potential accuracy problems; review monthly standard deviations for changes in random errors or imprecision.

- Correlate these QC changes with other performance data, such as results from proficiency testing surveys, comparison of methods results with real patient samples, changes in reagents, and changes in calibrations. Investigate problems and recommend corrective actions, such as recalibration, increased maintenance, and additional operator training. Make improvements in the testing process when possible.

- Periodically assess whether the QC design is still appropriate based on the routine performance being observed.

How do you decide what control rules and number of control measurements should be used?

Many laboratories just use 2s or 3s control limits, but we don't recommend that practice. The use of 2s control limits leads to too many false rejections, e.g., 5% for N=1, 10% for N=2, 14% for N=3. The use of 3s control limits may not provide enough error detection. Because of this, laboratory QC needs to be carefully planned. The control rules and number of control measurements should be designed or selected for the particular test and method, taking into account the quality required for the test and the performance observed for the method. Guidelines for doing this will be provided in the next chapter. Quantitative methodology is available in the literature [6] and described on Westgard Web: see www.westgard.com/lesson52.htm.

Isn't there another approach besides statistical QC?

The advantage of statistical QC is that it provides a widely applicable technique that can monitor the entire analytical process. Other techniques may monitor individual steps in the process or individual components in an instrument system. That makes it possible to establish a set of individual QC procedures that will check all the individual steps and individual components that might cause errors. That approach may be referred to as a quality system.

- **D5441** *NCCLS EP-18, "Quality Management for Unit-Use Testing,"* *provides guidance for identifying test system, environmental, and operator sources of error. Many manufacturers adhere to this NCCLS guidance and have identified potential sources of error for their test system. Manufacturers should provide this information to their client laboratories upon request.*

- This EP-18 document [7] provides a large table "Example of System-Specific Sources or Errors Matrix" that covers the total testing process and includes sections on specimen collection, sample presentation, instrument/reagents, results/readout/raw data, preliminary review, and integration/report into chart.
- The idea is that a manufacturer would identify those possible sources of error for a given analytic system and suggest a method of monitoring that source. Typical methods of monitoring include specific instrument checks, periodic quality control, split sample analysis, electronic tests, proficiency testing, delta checks, environmental monitoring, clinical surveillance, error and incident reporting, and auditing. The recommendation for monitoring analysts and operators often is training and competency assessment.

Who's responsible for QC in the laboratory?

QC planning should be the responsibility of laboratory management, usually the director, manager, or quality specialist. The medical director has a critical role in defining the quality requirements for the laboratory. The actual QC planning function may then be delegated to a manager or quality specialist. Implementation is usually delegated to supervisors and technologists who are in charge of managing specified analytical systems and testing processes. Routine operation is delegated to everyone who performs a laboratory test.

In large laboratories, there may be several quality specialists who spend a large part of their time dealing with quality systems. In small laboratories, the most senior technologist may inherit the responsibilities for quality. In point-of-care situations, the central laboratory may be responsible for the implementation, training, and maintenance of quality systems, but each healthcare worker who performs a test should be accountable for routine QC operations.

What not to do?

Many current QC practices in laboratories are less than optimal, contribute to today's problems with statistical QC, and compromise the practical usefulness of QC in routine applications. We know many of the points listed below go against the grain of current practice.

- **DON'T use 2 SD control limits!** Probably well over half of laboratories worldwide use control limits that are calculated as the mean plus and minus 2 standard deviations (SD), also known as a 1_{2s} rule. This practice is known to have a high level of false rejections – 1 out of every 20 points is expected to exceed 2 SD limits, which is a 5% rate of false rejection. However, many laboratorians don't understand that when two controls are analyzed per run, the false rejections rate is 10%, with three controls per run it's up to 14%, and with four controls per run it's about 18%. This false rejection rate can potentially cause a 10 to 20% waste of laboratory resources! Certainly the use of 2 SD control limits should be avoided with any automated analytical system. However, since customers aren't demanding such a change, manufacturers continue to support the use of 2 SD limits in their QC software. Marketing responds to customer "wants," rather than the real "needs" for better QC procedures with lower false rejection rates. Wants and needs are not necessarily the same!
- **DON'T just repeat the controls!** In many laboratories, the common response to an out-of-control situation is just to repeat the controls, rather than to fix the problem. The rationale is that the out-of-control situation is likely a false rejection, therefore, let's check again. And often if the repeats are still out, the response is to prepare new controls for analysis. And, of course, if they're out, they will also be repeated.The problem with this practice is that you're actually changing the control rules and are requiring that two or more consecutive points exceed a 2 SD limit (e.g., 2_{2s}, 3_{2s}, even 4_{2s}).

While this change in rules does reduce false rejections, it also reduces the error detection, leading to a practice that has little chance of detecting medically important errors.

- **DON'T use the same control rules for all tests!** If we need to eliminate 2 SD control limits, should we use 3 SD limits or possibly multirule QC instead? First of all, there's no *one* rule or one *set* of rules that's right for *all* tests and methods. Some methods have better precision than others, therefore different QC procedures should be used. The most cost-effective operation is possible when the QC procedures are selected for the individual tests on the basis of the quality required for the test and the performance observed for the method [6].

- **DON'T use bottle values to calculate control limits!** The basic principle of statistical QC is to assess current performance relative to past performance. The critical measures of past performance are the mean and SD observed for the control material analyzed by your method in your laboratory. Bottle values generally reflect the overall performance of a group of laboratories, and while the bottle value means may be useful for assessing the accuracy of your methods, the bottle value SDs are usually larger and will give control limits that are too wide (which causes low error detection).

- **DON'T use medical decision limits as control limits!** Another ill-advised practice is the use of "medical decision limits" to transfer medical quality requirements directly to a control chart, which supposedly eliminates statistical rejections and only identifies problems that are medically important. Again, the technique is appealing because it provides wider control limits, which give fewer false rejections, but it also causes lower error detection. [See the Myth of Medical Decision Limits: www.westgard.com/essay8.htm.]

- **DON'T rely on electronic QC alone!** Alternatives to statistical QC are desirable, particularly in Point-of-Care (POC) applications where personnel may have little laboratory background or training. Electronic QC is appealing because of its simplicity, low cost, and few rejections. Unfortunately, electronic QC checks only a few steps in the total testing process – often only the electronic readout step. Therefore, electronic QC by itself is not sufficient to assure the quality of the tests being performed. [See Electronic QC and the Total Testing Process: www.westgard.com/essay17.htm.]

- **DON'T eliminate statistical QC in POC applications!** Statistical QC can monitor many steps in the analytical process, including the proficiency of the operator. Statistical QC should be considered essential whenever operator skills may affect the results of the testing process.

What to do?

Many of the problems identified above have been addressed by the QC practice guidelines [C24-A2, 4] that were published in early 1999 by the National Committee for Clinical Laboratory Standards (NCCLS). These guidelines draw heavily on recommendations by a European working group [8], thus there are some common practice guidelines emerging in both the European and American markets. Some of the important principles are summarized by the list of DO's that follows.

- **DO calculate control limits from your own laboratory data!** The NCCLS C24-A2 document makes it very clear that "the mean and standard deviation of a control material should be established on the basis of repeated measurements on those materials by the methods in use in the laboratory." It further recommends the use of cumulative control limits that are based on the means and SDs for several months of laboratory data.
- **DO select QC procedures that minimize false rejections!** It's best to keep the chance of false rejections below 5%. This requires that you eliminate the use of 2 SD control limits whenever the number of control measurements (N) is more than 1, which implies you should almost NEVER use 2 SD limits. Use of 3 SD limits will give you only a 1% false rejection rate when N is 2 to 4. Multirule combinations will usually have between 2 to 4% false rejects as long as N is 2 to 4. When higher

Ns from 5 to 8 are used to achieve greater error detection, false rejections of 6 to 8% may have to be tolerated.

- **DO reject out-of-control runs, identify the problem, and eliminate the cause!** When QC procedures have been carefully selected to minimize false rejection and maximize detection of medically important errors, the proper response to an out-of-control signal is to reject the analytical run, trouble-shoot the method, identify the problem, eliminate the cause of the problem, and verify the test results for patient specimens.

- **DO standardize QC operations!** QC applications themselves must be systematic from the preparation of control materials through the interpretation of control results. Automatic preparation, scheduling, and sampling of control materials is important for standardizing the collection of control data. Computer implementation of control rules is important for standardizing the interpretation of control data.

- **DO provide computer support to analyze and interpret QC data!** Computer support will facilitate data calculations, such as the calculation of cumulative means, SDs, and control limits. More important, computer support is necessary to individualize the QC procedure for each laboratory test. In addition, online computer support is desirable for interpretation of control data for tests performed by high-volume multitest analyzers or any analyzer operated by personnel with limited laboratory background and training. Computer support is also essential for complex QC designs, such as multi-stage QC procedures that utilize a "startup" set of rules for high error detection and a "monitor" set of rules for low false rejections, with periodic switching between the two designs as appropriate during the operating cycle of an analyzer.

- **DO select QC procedures that detect medically important errors!** A practical goal is to aim for a 90% chance of detecting medically important errors. QC procedures that have appropriate error detection can be selected on the basis of the quality required for the test and the imprecision and inaccuracy observed for the method. The NCCLS C24-A2 document describes the general steps for planning a QC procedure (in section 5), which include (a) defining a quality requirement for the test, (b) determining the imprecision and bias of the method, (c) identifying candidate QC procedures, (d) predicting QC performance, i.e., assessing the rejection characteristics of the candidate QC procedures, (e) setting criteria for QC performance, and (f) selecting the appropriate control rules and number of control measurements.

- **DO adopt a Total QC strategy to maximize the cost-effectiveness of QC!** The Total QC system is a mix of statistical QC, instrument checks, validation tests, preventive maintenance, and patient-data QC procedures [12]. The optimum mix can be defined on the basis of the error detection available by statistical QC. If 90% error detection can be achieved, then the Total QC strategy should rely on statistical QC to detect problems; the time and effort spent on other QC procedures should be minimized. When 90% error detection cannot be achieved, then the Total QC strategy should be to increase the use of non-statistical procedures and components, including increased preventive maintenance, increased operator training, and reduced rotations of operators. [See Total QC Strategies – www.westgard.com/lesson8.htm.]

References

1. Westgard JO. Basic QC Practices, 2nd ed. Madison WI:Westgard QC, Inc., 2003.

2. US Centers for Medicare & Medicaid Services (CMS). Medicare, Medicaid, and CLIA Programs: Laboratory Requirements Relating to quality Systems and Certain Personnel Qualifications. Final Rule. Fed Regist Jan 24 2003;16:3640-3714.

3. CMS State Operations Manual – Interpretive Guidelines: Appendix C. www.cms.gov/clia/appendc.asp

4. NCCLS C24-A2. Statistical quality control for quantitative measurements: Principles and definitions; Approved guideline - Second edition. National Committee for Clinical Laboratory Standards, 940 West Valley Road, Wayne, PA 19087, USA, 1999.

5. Westgard JO, Barry PL, Hunt MR, Groth T. A multi-rule Shewhart chart for quality control in clinical chemistry. Clin Chem 1981;27:493-501.

6. Westgard JO. Internal quality control: Planning and implementation strategies. Ann Clin Biochem 2003;40:593-611.

7. NCCLS EP-18A. Quality management for unit-use testing; Approved guideline. National Committee for Clinical Laboratory Standards, 940 West Valley Road, Wayne, PA 19087 USA, 2002.

8. Hyltoft Petersen P, Ricos C, Stockl D, Libeer JC, Baadenhuijsen H. Fraser C, Thienpont L. Proposed guidelines for the internal quality control of analytical results in the medical laboratory. Eur J Clin Chem Clin Biochem 1996;34:983-999.

13: Doing the Right QC

In principle, the CLIA regulations require that laboratories perform the amount of QC that is appropriate for the methods in use in the laboratory. That's the real meaning of §493.1256 [1] and the following rules:

(a) QC should monitor the accuracy and precision of the complete analytic process;

(b) The laboratory should establish the number, type, and frequency of testing control materials;

(c) QC should detect immediate errors that occur due to test system failure, adverse environmental conditions, and operator performance;

These rules provide good guidance for assuring the quality of laboratory test results, but CLIA continues to provide minimum requirements for compliance:

- Run two controls for quantitative tests each day when patient specimens are assayed or examined (note that this general requirement may be modified by specific requirements in specialty areas as described in sections §493.1261 through §493.1278, e.g., blood gas analysis requires 1 control every 8 hours, hematology manual cell counts require 1 control every 8 hours, non-manual coagulation requires 2 levels of control every 8 hours, but manual coagulation tests require 2 levels of control each time specimens are analyzed, etc.);

The danger in the regulations is that laboratories can be in compliance with the minimum requirements, yet not assure the quality of patient test results. Compliance with the minimum QC does not assure that the laboratory will utilize the proper number of control materials and the proper frequency of testing to detect immediate errors. Concern for patient safety should make quality a higher priority than compliance!

Quality vs Compliance

Section 493.1256 is the Standard for Control Procedures and provides the details for control procedures. Parts a through c2 describe a laboratory's responsibilities for assuring the quality of patient test results.

(a) "The laboratory is responsible for having control procedures that monitor the accuracy and precision of the complete analytical process."

"Complete analytical process" – a new phrase that appears in the Final Rule – implies several steps that include sample introduction and manipulation, reagent additions, generation of the analytical reaction that is measured, measurement of the analyte via some type of sensor, and conversion of the sensor response to an analytical result. The obvious approach for monitoring precision and accuracy is to use liquid controls that go through the complete analytical process just like a real patient sample. Routine calculation of the internal QC data will provide ongoing estimates of method precision (SD, CV) and indications of any systematic changes or drifts (stability of mean or changes over time).

Given that liquid controls are needed to monitor the complete analytical process, there should be concern that Electronic QC (EQC) is not adequate. Here's where the State Inspectors Manual and "equivalent QC procedures" become important. We'll discuss this in detail in the next chapter.

(b) "The laboratory must establish the number, type, and frequency of testing control materials using, if applicable, the performance specifications verified or established by the laboratory..."

Here's where the fun begins. It is generally accepted as good laboratory practice to analyze two or three different control materials whose mean values are close to concentrations important for the interpretation of the test results. The type of material will usually depend on what is available commercially. Whether assayed or unassayed, a laboratory should establish its own mean and SD (or CV) from measurements carried out under routine operating conditions. The act of establishing your own means and SDs brings in the performance specifications observed in your own laboratory.

The total number of control measurements needed for QC purposes depends on the quality required for the test, the precision and accuracy observed for the method, and the statistical control rules that are implemented. There is a step-by-step process for planning QC procedures that takes all these factors into account [2]. We'll walk you through a simplified form of this process in the "Issues and Answers" section of this chapter.

The frequency of testing control materials should be related to the stability of the process and its susceptibility to problems. It makes sense to analyze control materials more frequently if a method is unstable. One practical indication of stability is the frequency of calibration. Whenever a method is calibrated, it also makes sense to run controls to check performance. Susceptibility is often related to the level of automation of the analytical procedure. Manual methods are usually much more susceptible to problems than automated methods; early generations of automation are more susceptible to problems than later generations of automation. However, there is no quantitative methodology that tells you the frequency for running controls. It is a judgment that should be based on manufacturer's recommendations for stability and your expectation of susceptibility, based on your experience with the methods in your laboratory, the skills of your analysts, and the factors and variables that change in your laboratory.

(c 1) The control procedures must detect immediate errors that occur due to test system failure, adverse environmental conditions, and operator performance.

Here's where you have some new and serious responsibility! The intent of these regulations is not just for laboratories to run controls, but to be able to "detect immediate errors." This phrase "detect immediate errors" has never appeared in earlier versions of CLIA, therefore it will need some clarification and explanation.

- Error does not mean *all* errors, but those that are medically important. All tests are in error to some degree because all methods have some imprecision or random error. It is important to be able to detect errors of a size that would cause test results to be misinterpreted and therefore cause patients to be misdiagnosed or mistreated. You can calculate the size of medically important errors if you define the quality required for a test and assess the precision and accuracy available from a method.

- Immediate is not a type of error! It means that laboratories should detect important errors immediately. That requires controls to be analyzed at an appropriate frequency, the proper number of control measurements be collected, and the appropriate control rules be used to interpret the data. Patient data algorithms can also be utilized to cross check between tests and to measure the "average of normals" (Aon) to monitor stability [3].

The most obvious implication is that analyzing controls once a day or once a shift may not be good practice, even though CLIA may specify those minimums for compliance. If the laboratory has an instrument that is reporting data continuously throughout an eight hour shift, the ability to "detect immediate errors" depends on analyzing controls throughout that shift, not just at the beginning or at the end.

An appropriate strategy for dealing with this requirement is to utilize what we call "multistage QC." Begin with a "startup design" that provides high detection of medically important errors, then switch to a "monitor design" for periodic verification during the ongoing run and reporting of results. A third stage can be employed using patient data, such as an "Average of normals" (Aon) algorithms to monitor stability and determine when controls should be analyzed again to validate method performance [4].

A useful analogy is the QC done on an airplane. There certainly is a "startup" design that is employed while the plane is on the ground. It's very detailed and thorough and has the objective of catching any little problem *before* you're up and flying. Once in the air, there is a "monitor design" that follows critical factors and variables to ensure the flight remains safe. We can and should do multistage QC in the laboratory.

(c 2) Monitor over time the accuracy and precision of test performance that may be influenced by changes in test system performance, environmental conditions, and variance in operator performance.

The emphasis here is "monitor over time" in contrast to the "detect immediate errors" in the previous statement. The obvious strategy here is to participate in a peer-comparison program that gives you information on the performance of your method over time, as well as the comparative performance of other laboratories using the same control materials. Laboratories can utilize the same control data being collected to "detect immediate errors," but analyze that data for monthly periods.

Changes in the precision of your methods will show up in the monthly and cumulative summaries of your method SDs and CVs. Any changes with the accuracy of your methods will show up in the monthly and cumulative comparison of your mean values with those of the peer group. If there are any problems with the control materials themselves, they will show up in the peer comparison data.

Issues and Answers

What QC is right for your methods?

The problem is to figure out the right QC based on the accuracy and precision of the method, the number of control materials to be tested, and the size of the errors that are medically important and need to be detected immediately. That QC procedure can be identified by following a QC selection process that considers the quality required for the test, the precision and accuracy observed for the method, and rejection characteristics of the particular control rules and number of control measurements used by the QC procedure. The answer is not a "one size fits all" rule or set of rules, but a process that leads to the right rule or rules for an individual test and method. In this discussion, we're going to break this process down into several steps:

- How do you characterize the performance of your method?
- What size errors are medically important?
- What size errors can be detected by a QC procedure?
- What QC is right for methods with different Sigma metrics?

- How can you document the appropriateness of your QC procedures?

How do you characterize the performance of your method?

A simple approach is to calculate the Sigma metric for your method, as discussed earlier in Chapter 10, following these steps:

- Define the quality required for the test, starting with the CLIA criterion for acceptable performance in proficiency testing, which defines the allowable total error (TE_a) for individual tests;
- Determine the precision (SD) and accuracy (bias) of your method from initial evaluation studies, such as the replication and comparison of methods experiments, or from ongoing data from routine QC to estimate the method SD and proficiency testing or peer comparison data to estimate the method bias;
- Calculate the Sigma metric for your method as follows:

$$\textbf{Sigma} = (\mathbf{TE_a} - \textbf{bias})/\textbf{SD}$$

For cholesterol, for example, the CLIA criterion is an allowable total error of 10%. If your method has a CV of 2.0% and a bias of 1.0%, then the Sigma metric for your method is 4.5 [(10-1)/2]. In interpreting the method Sigma metric, remember that the higher the Sigma value, the better the method performance. Established performance benchmarks are as follows:

- Sigma of 6.0 is the goal for world class quality;
- Sigma of 3.0 is the minimum allowable Sigma for routine production.

For sources of the numbers in the Sigma calculation, the CLIA proficiency testing criteria can be found in the CLIA regulations as included here in Appendix 1. For figures for the method SD and bias, CLIA requires that you verify the manufacturer's claims for precision and accuracy for any method introduced after April 24, 2003, thus there should be data on the method SD and bias available in your own laboratory from your initial replication (SD) and comparison experiments (bias vs comparative method), respectively, or from ongoing estimates from your routine QC data (SD) and periodic peer comparison of proficiency testing surveys (bias vs mean of group). Alternatively, as a starting point, you can begin with the manufacturer's claims for precision and accuracy, which must be available to you before any method or system can be marketed and sold.

To demonstrate the usefulness of calculating method's Sigma performance, here are the different QC procedures that are appropriate for methods with different Sigma metrics:

- *When your method Sigma is 6 or greater, you can do QC anyway you want, just be sure to keep the false rejections low by using wide control limits – at least 3s.*
- *When your method Sigma is 5 or so, use N=2 or 3 with 2.5s or 3.0s control limits.*
- *When your method Sigma is 4 or so, increase N to 4 to 6 and use either the $1_{2.5s}$ single rule or a $1_{3s}/2_{2s}/R_{4s}/4_{1s}$ multirule procedure.*
- *With method Sigmas below 4.0, run all the control you can afford. In addition, increase the frequency of instrument function checks, performance validation checks, and preventive maintenance.*
- *With method Sigmas below 3.0, look for a new and better method. You can't do enough QC to assure the quality of the test results from methods having less than 3.0 Sigma performance!*

Once you know the Sigma metrics for your methods, the above guidelines will give you a pretty good idea of what QC is right for those methods. If you want to understand the rationale for these guidelines, keep reading.

What size errors are medically important?

All test results are in error to some extent due to the inherent random error caused by the stable imprecision of the method. *If a method has an SD, then there will be some error in the test results!*

A. Calculate Method Sigma

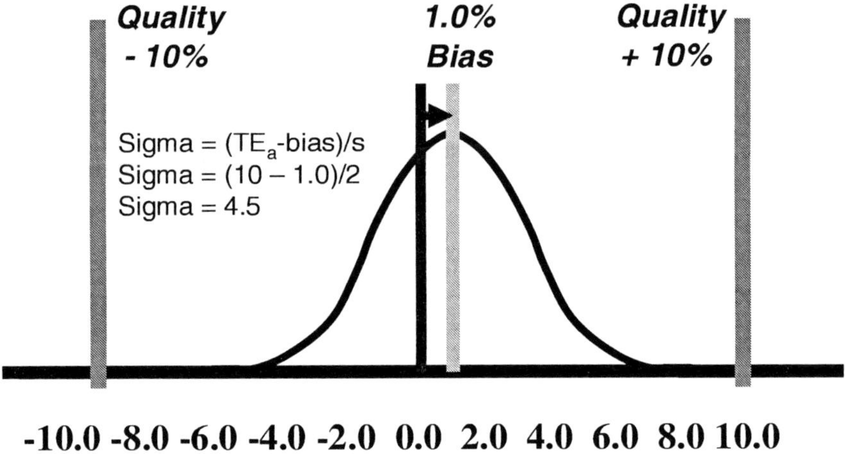

B. Calculate Medically Important SE

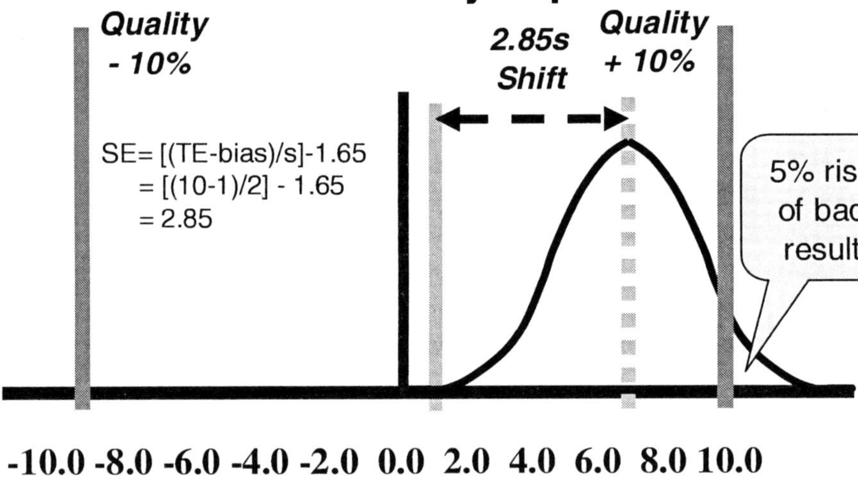

Inaccuracy can ideally be reduced to zero, but imprecision will always exist, thus test results will always have some analytical error. The real issue is the size of an error that becomes medically important and needs to be detected by the QC procedure. For automated systems, we are most concerned with the systematic errors that occur due to deterioration of instrument components and changes in reagents, operators, and operating conditions.

The graphic here shows the relationship between the Sigma Metric for method performance (top part A) and the Sigma Metric for QC Design (bottom part B), which is the medically important systematic error that needs to be detected by the QC procedure. We call this the "critical SE" and have used the abbreviation "delta SE critical" (ΔSE_{crit}) in many discussions on Westgard Web and in our training materials on QC design and planning. The calculation of the medically important systematic error is based on limiting the "risk" for producing a bad test result to 5%, which means that the area in tail is defined as a z-value of 1.65s, thus providing the following equation:

$$\mathbf{\Delta SE_{crit} = [(TE_a - bias)/s] - 1.65s}$$

We consider ΔSE_{crit} as the "QC design metric" for quality control [2]. It is a Sigma metric because it describes the medically important systematic error as a multiple of the method SD. For example, a critical SE of 3.0s means that it is important to detect a systematic shift equivalent to 3.0 times the method SD. If the method SD is 2.0 mg/dL, then the critical shift amounts to 6.0 mg/dL. If the method CV is 2.0%, the critical shift is 6.0%, which can be converted to concentration units at a critical decision concentration.

For our cholesterol example, where TE_a is 10%, bias is 1.0%, and SD is 2.0%, the medically important systematic error is 2.85s, i.e., a systematic shift equivalent to 2.85 times the standard deviation of the method needs to be detected by the QC procedure to assure the desired quality will be produced for a cholesterol test.

Note that the equation for the QC design metric could also be written as follows:

$$\mathbf{\Delta SE_{crit} = Method\ Sigma - 1.65s}$$

That means that the requirement for the QC procedure is directly related to the Sigma performance of the method, i.e., the higher the method Sigma, the larger the size of the systematic error that needs to be detected by the QC procedure. The larger the error, the easier it is for the QC procedure to detect the error!

What size errors can be detected by a QC procedure?

While it's easy to calculate the Sigma metric to describe the performance of a method in your own laboratory and also to calculate the medically important systematic error (QC design metric) that must be detected by the QC procedure, most laboratories don't know the error detection capabilities of their QC procedures. Fortunately this information has been available in the scientific literature for many years [5,6].

The performance of a QC procedure can be described by two characteristics:

- Probability for error detection (P_{ed}), which describes the probability of seeing a rejection signal when there is a change in the precision or accuracy of the analytical method;
- Probability for false rejection (P_{fr}), which describes the probability of seeing a rejection signal when there is no change in method performance, except for the inherent imprecision of the method.

Ideally, P_{ed} should be high, near 1.00 to provide a 100% chance of detecting a medically important analytical error. Ideally, P_{fr} should be low, near 0.00 to provide a 0.0% chance of false rejections that would otherwise waste time and effort and slow the reporting of patient test results.

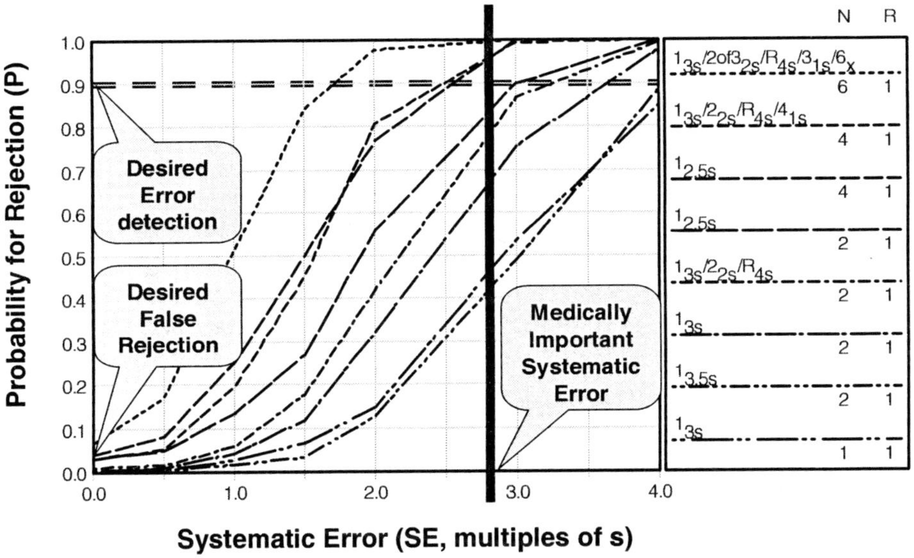

These probabilities can be described graphically using a "power function graph" [5], as shown above. Note that there are 8 power curves here, each corresponding to specific control rules and a specific number of control measurements, as shown in the key at the right side. We generally set the desired error detection at 0.90 (y-axis, probability for rejection), as shown by the dashed horizontal line, which shows that the capability of the QC procedure to achieve that performance depends on the size of the error to be detected (x-axis, systematic error). The vertical line shows the size of the medically important systematic error for our cholesterol example (2.85s). Note that only the top 3 QC procedures on the list in the key provide the desired error detection. Of these 3, the 2nd and 3rd down the list require 4 control measurements and are therefore less costly than the 1st on the list, which requires 6 control measurements. Note also that the probability for false rejection will be lower for the N=4 QC procedures.

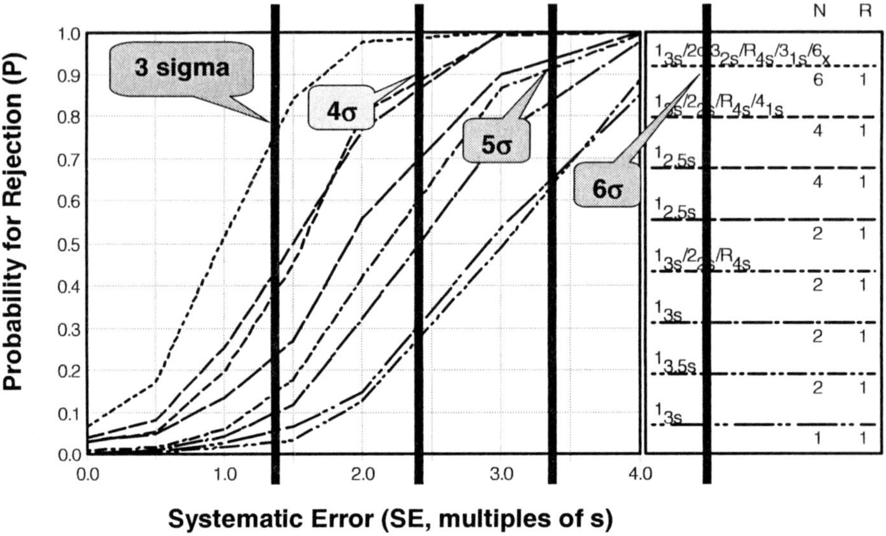

What QC is appropriate for methods with different Sigma metrics?

Since the medically important systematic error is directly dependent on the Sigma metric of the method, it follows that the QC procedure that is appropriate must also be related to the Sigma metric of the method. A quantitative description of the relationship is provided in the accompanying figure, which shows a "Sigma scale" imposed on the power function graph and vertical lines corresponding, from left to right, to 3, 4, 5, and 6 Sigma (the latter being slightly off-scale at the right).

Given a method with 3 Sigma performance (leftmost vertical line), a laboratory needs to do all the QC it can afford. Even a multirule QC procedure with 6 controls per run will have difficulty providing the desired error detection.

On the other hand, a method having 6 Sigma performance (rightmost vertical line) can be QC'd by any of these rules, certainly 1_{3s} with N=2 and even 1_{3s} with N=1. Given that CLIA requires a minimum of 2 levels of controls, a laboratory could even use a $1_{3.5s}$ rule with N=2 to effectively reduce false rejections to zero and still maintain the desired error detection.

For a method with 5 Sigma performance, 2 levels with either a $1_{3s}/2_{2s}/R_{4s}$ multirule or a $1_{2.5s}$ single rule would be appropriate. For a method with 4 Sigma performance, it will be necessary to increase N to 4, which means analyzing each of the two levels of controls twice to get the total 4 measurements that are needed.

In summary, when your method Sigma is 6 or greater, you can do QC anyway you want, just be sure to keep the false rejections low by using wide control limits – at least 3s. When your method Sigma is 5 or so, use N=2 or 3 with 2.5s or 3.0s control limits. When your method Sigma is 4 or so, increase N to 4 or 6 and use either the $1_{2.5s}$ single rule or a $1_{3s}/2_{2s}/R_{4s}/4_{1s}$ multirule procedure. With method Sigmas below 4.0, run all the control you can afford. In addition, increase the frequency of instrument function checks, performance validation checks, and preventive maintenance. With method Sigmas below 3.0, look for a new and better method.

For a more quantitative QC selection process that is supported by computer tools, see the recent publication on "Internal Quality Control Planning and Implementation Strategies" [6] which is available free on the Internet.

How can you document the "rightness" of your QC procedures?

When the inspector comes calling on your laboratory, you can demonstrate the appropriateness of your QC procedures with the calculations and graphs discussed here. This documentation is readily available with the EZ Rules® computer program [7], which provides the Sigma metric calculations and graphics. This program also provides an automatic selection function that will search for the optimal control rules and number of control measurements based on your entries for the quality requirement, observed imprecision, and observed inaccuracy. The program also allows you to use biologic goals and medically important changes (clinical decision intervals) as quality requirements.

What are some examples of method Sigmas and appropriate QC procedures?

(a) Cholesterol with method CV of 3.0% and bias of 1.0% is 3.0 Sigma [(10-1)/3];

(b) Cholesterol with method CV of 2.0% and bias of 2.0% is 4.0 Sigma [(10-2)/2];

(c) Glucose with method CV of 2.0% and bias of 0.0% is 5.0 Sigma [(10-0)/2]; and

(d) pH with method SD of 0.005 pH unit and bias of 0.01 pH unit is 6.0 Sigma [(0.04-0.01)/0.005].

And the appropriate QC procedures are:

(a) All the QC you can afford;

(b) Use 2.5s limits for a single rule or a multirule procedure having $1_{3s}/2_{2s}/R_{4s}/4_{1s}$ with a total N of at least 4, which means making duplicate measurements on each of two different levels of materials,

(c) Use an N of 2 with 2.5s or 3.0s for a single rule procedure, or a simple multirule having $1_{3s}/2_{2s}/R_{4s}$ rules.

(d) Do QC anyway you want, just be sure to keep the N low and the control limits wide to minimize cost.

DO's and DON'Ts

- DO take your responsibility for quality seriously, which means providing the right QC for the tests and methods in your laboratory.
- DO start with the CLIA PT criteria for acceptable performance for the initial definitions of requirements for analytical quality. Remember that these criteria are allowable total errors, which are the same as tolerance limits in Six Sigma terminology.

- DO use Sigma metrics to characterize method performance relative to the quality required for the test.
- DO utilize method validation studies for your initial estimates of the method SD or CV (from the replication experiment) and method bias (from comparison of methods experiment).
- DON'T get hung up on the estimate of bias. You can initially assume a bias of zero, which will give an optimistic estimate of the Sigma metric for a method. You can refine the estimate of the Sigma metric on the basis of ongoing estimates of method bias from peer-comparison surveys or proficiency testing surveys.
- DO start with the simple graphic QC selection tool provided here, i.e., the Sigma metrics critical-error graph on page 168.
- DO get more instruction and training in Six Sigma Quality Management and analytical applications for method performance and QC.

References

1. CLIA Final Rules. U.S. Department of Health and Human Services. Medicare, Medicaid and CLIA Programs: Laboratory requirements relating to quality systems and certain personnel qualifications. Final rule. Fed Regist 2003;68:3640-714 (available at http://www.phppo.cdc.gov/clia/pdf/CMS-2226-F.pdf)
2. Westgard JO. Internal quality control: planning and implementation. Ann Clin Biochem 2003;40:593-611. Available on the Internet at www.westgard.com/iqcpaper2003.html
3. Westgard JO, Smith FA, Mountain PJ, Boss S. Design and assessment of average of normals (AON) patient data algorithms to maximize run lengths for automatic process control. Clin Chem 1996;42:1683-1688.

4. Westgard JO. Six Sigma Quality Design and Control: Desirable precision and requisite QC for laboratory measurement processes. Chapter 12. Multi-Stage Quality Control. Madison, WI: Westgard QC, Inc., 2001.

5. Westgard JO, Groth T, Aronsson T, Falk H, deVerdier C-H. Performance characteristics of rules for internal quality control: Probabilities for false rejection and error detection. Clin Chem 1977;23:1857-1867.

6. Westgard JO, Groth T. Power function graphs for statistical control rules. Clin Chem 1979;25:863-869.

7. Westgard JO. Validator EZ Rules Program: Automatic selection of statistical control rules for laboratory tests. Madison WI:Westgard QC, Inc., 2000. (see www.westgard.com/ezrules.htm)

14: ?Equivalent QC Procedures?

One of the biggest changes in the CLIA Final Rule is actually found in the CMS Interpretive Guidelines in the form of recommendations for "*Equivalent QC Procedures*." These procedures allow further reductions from daily QC to weekly or even monthly QC for certain analytic systems that contain internal procedural controls. Given that QC is one of the major deficiencies cited in laboratory inspections, it is difficult to understand the rationale for *reducing* QC from the already low minimum of two levels of control per day.

CMS uses the term "internal procedural control" to identify a monitoring check or system that the manufacturer builds into an instrument. The most common is an electronic check on the instrument readout, which is often referred to as Electronic QC (EQC). CMS often uses the abbreviation EQC for equivalent QC procedures, but we prefer to identify Equivalent QC procedures as Eqc to distinguish them from EQC. However, we think the CMS abbreviation reveals the underlying purpose of these guidelines – Eqc provides an allowance for EQC in Near Patient Testing and Point-of-Care applications.

As part of the Eqc guidelines, CMS provides "evaluation protocols" by which a laboratory can qualify an instrument for reduced QC. These evaluation protocols involve running external controls daily for a period of 10 days (option 1) or 30 days (option 2) or 60 days (option 3). The condition for qualification is the absence of any out-of-control signals from both the internal procedural controls and the external controls during the evaluation period.

It seems contradictory to demand that testing sites follow a QC protocol to qualify for reductions in QC, given that deficiencies in QC are the most common problem in those very same sites where Eqc options are likely to be implemented. If these sites can't, don't, or won't perform QC properly, then the evaluation protocols recommended by CMS are inherently limited and the validity of Eqc options is questionable.

Eqc points out the difference between the spirit of the CLIA law and the letter of the Interpretive Guidelines. Because of the controversial nature of the Eqc options [1], it is important to review the exact language in the CLIA Rules and the CMS Interpretive Guidelines, which requires extensive quotations from the CLIA Final Rule [2] and the State Operations Manual [3].

The Final Rules

§493.1256 Standard: Control procedures. [2]

(a) For each test system, the laboratory is responsible for having control procedures that monitor the accuracy and precision of the complete analytic process.

(b) The laboratory must establish the number, type, and frequency of testing control materials using, if applicable, the performance specifications verified or established by the laboratory as specified in §493.1253(b)(3).

(c) The control procedure must (1) detect immediate errors that occur due to test system failure, adverse environmental conditions, and operator performance. (2) Monitor over time the accuracy and precision of test performance that may be influenced by changes in test system performance and environmental conditions, and variance in operator performance.

***(d) Unless CMS approves a procedure, specified in Appendix C of the State Operations Manual (CMS Pub. 7), that provides equivalent quality testing,* the laboratory must (1) perform control procedures as defined in this section unless otherwise specified in the additional specialty and subspecialty requirements at §493.1261 through 493.1278. (2) For each test system, perform control procedures using the number and frequency specified by the manufacturer or established by the laboratory when they meet or exceed the requirements in paragraph (d)(3) of this section.**

The underlined text – *Unless CMS approves a procedure, specified in Appendix C of the State Operations Manual (CMS Pub. 7), that provides equivalent quality testing* – is the focus of our discussion. Here's where the spirit of the law and the letter of the Interpretive Guidelines provide conflicting requirements for laboratory QC.

CMS Interpretive Guideline [2]

D5444 Interpretive Guidelines 493.1256(d)

Considerations for establishing equivalent quality testing
If the laboratory chooses to implement the reduced QC frequency for multiple instruments (including the same make and model used to perform the same test) a successful evaluation process must be performed for each instrument for which the (QC) frequency applies.

Note: *The regulations require laboratories to follow test system manufacturer's instruction for performing the testing. This means the laboratory must perform and follow the manufacturer's package insert as approved or cleared by the FDA.*

Advancements in laboratory technology have led to test systems that often include internal monitoring systems (electronic, internal, procedural controls, etc). Electronic controls only monitor the electrical or electronic components of the test system. Internal or procedural controls may only monitor a portion of the analytic process, such as sample addition, instrument/reagents interaction, or test completion. These advancements may allow laboratories flexibility in determining control procedures that provide equivalent quality procedures to the traditional daily testing of two levels of external control materials. However, under no circumstances may the laboratory reduce the frequency of testing external control materials to less than that specified by the manufacturer's test system instructions.

Note: *Since the purpose of control testing is to detect immediate errors and monitor performance over time, increasing the interval between control testing (i.e., weekly, or monthly) will require a more extensive evaluation of patient test results when a control failure occurs (see §493.1282). The director must consider the laboratory's clinical and legal responsibility for providing accurate and reliable patient test results versus the cost implications of reducing the quality control testing frequency.*

Identifying Sources of Errors
As a first step, the laboratory must determine the test system's sources of error. The test system instructions (product insert) may contain this information. If this information is not provided, the

laboratory should contact the manufacturer to obtain this information in writing and include it in the procedure manual.

Test Systems with Internal and/or Procedural Controls
If internal or procedural controls are provided as part of the test system, the following information must be determined in the laboratory:

- *Whether the internal/procedural control(s) monitor all components of the test system. This information may be included in the package insert. If not, the laboratory must contact the test system's manufacturer to obtain written documentation identifying the components of the test system monitored by the internal/procedural controls and include this information in the laboratory's procedure manual.*
- *If all components are not monitored, identify those components of the test system that are monitored by the internal/procedural control(s);*
- *Have a mechanism for monitoring those components of the test system <u>not</u> monitored by the internal/procedural control(s); and*
- *Evaluate the affect of adverse environmental conditions and the influence of operator variance and techniques.*

Note: *Although manufacturers may assist laboratories by providing quality control instructions, the laboratory is ultimately responsible for the performance of appropriate quality control procedures, including the documentation and interpretation of quality control data. Under subpart M, the director is responsible for ensuring that quality control and quality assessment programs are established and maintained to assure the quality of laboratory services, including the identification of failures in quality as they occur.*

CMS Equivalent Quality Control Procedures

Three different Eqc options are described in **D5445** of the CMS Interpretive Guidelines, which are quoted directly here to provide a complete description.

The equivalent quality control procedures described below may only be used for laboratory testing subject to the following control procedure requirements:

- *§493.1256(d)(3)(i-iii) – control requirements for quantitative, qualitative and semi-quantitative procedures*
- *§493.1256(d)(3)(iv) – test procedures that include an extraction phase (limited to 1 and 2 below)*
- *§493.1257-493.1269 – control requirements for routine chemistry and hematology (limited to 1 and 2 below)*

As further technological advances are made and additional data becomes available, CMS will, as appropriate, revise the equivalent quality control procedures and/or the eligibility requirements for test procedures that may use equivalent quality control.

Option 1. Test Systems with Internal/Procedures Control(s) that Monitor the Entire Analytic Process.

If a test system uses one or more internal/procedural control(s) to monitor all of its analytic components and the laboratory using the test system successfully completes the evaluation process described below to demonstrate test system stability over time, the laboratory may use the equivalent quality control procedures described below in lieu of performing the applicable procedures specified in the regulations at §493.1256(d)(3)(i-iv) and the applicable specialty and subspecialty requirements listed for routine chemistry and hematology at §493.1267-493.1269.

Evaluation Process: *The laboratory must perform the test system's internal control procedure(s) in accordance with the manufacturer's instructions (but not less frequently than once each day of testing) and test two levels of external control material daily for 10 consecutive days of testing.*

- *If the internal and external control results are acceptable throughout the evaluation process, the laboratory may reduce the frequency of testing two levels of external control material from daily to* ***once per calendar month*** *unless the manufacturer requires more frequent and/or additional external control testing. The laboratory must continue to perform and monitor the* *internal control(s) in accordance with the manufacturer's instructions, but not less frequently than once each day of testing.*

- *If any internal or external control result is unacceptable during the evaluation process or after the laboratory has reduced the frequency for testing external control materials, the laboratory must repeat the unacceptable internal and/or external controls.*
  - *If the repeat control result(s) are within range, no further corrective action is necessary and the laboratory may, as applicable, resume the evaluation process or continue the reduced frequency of external control testing.*
  - *If the repeat control result(s) are not acceptable, the laboratory must identify the problem, take appropriate corrective action and follow the requirements at §493.1282(b)(2) before reporting patient test results. The laboratory must **restart** and successfully complete the evaluation process before reducing the frequency of testing external control materials.*
  - *All evaluation process and corrective action activities must be documented.*
- ***Note:** If a laboratory's existing QC data for the test system meets the evaluation process protocol described above, the laboratory may reduce the frequency for testing external control materials as specified above.*

Option 2. Test Systems with Internal/Procedures Control(s) that Monitor a Portion of the Analytic Process.

Some internal/procedure controls monitor only certain components of the test system. Although the test system's manufacturer may suggest other mechanisms to monitor the component(s) not checked by the internal/procedural controls, the laboratory is ultimately responsible for ensuring that all components of the analytic process are monitored. The laboratory may use the equivalent quality control procedures listed below in lieu of performing the applicable procedures specified in the regulations §493.1256(d)(3)(i-iv) and the applicable specialty and subspecialty requirements listed for routine chemistry and hematology at §493.1267-493.126, when it can demonstrate the test system's stability over time. This may be substantiated by successfully completing the evaluation process (described below).

Evaluation Process: *The laboratory must perform the test system's internal control procedure(s) in accordance with the manufacturer's instructions (but not less frequently than once each day of testing) and test two levels of external control material daily for **30** consecutive days of testing.*

- *If the internal and external control results are acceptable throughout the evaluation process, the laboratory may reduce the frequency of testing two levels of external control material from daily to **once per calendar week** unless the manufacturer requires more frequent and/or additional external control testing. The laboratory must continue to perform and monitor the internal control(s) in accordance with the manufacturer's instructions, but not less frequently than once each day of testing.*
- *[REST OF GUIDELINES ARE SAME AS FOR EARLIER OPTION 1.]*

Option 3. Test Systems without Internal/Procedures Control(s).

Test systems without internal/procedural controls subject to the extraction phase control requirements at §493.1256(d)(3)(iv) or the specialty or subspecialty requirements at §493.1261-493.1278 are not eligible for this option.

Advancements in laboratory technology have led to the production of test systems that are capable of maintaining stable performance specifications over time and are minimally influenced by adverse environmental conditions and operator variance. While the test system manufacturer should provide the laboratory with written documentation of the test system's stability (which may be included as part of the package insert or operator manual, and must be maintained by the laboratory), the laboratory is responsible for ensuring that all components of the analytic process are monitored. This may be accomplished by testing, at a minimum, two levels of external control material daily. The laboratory may use the equivalent quality control procedures described below in lieu of performing the applicable procedures specified in the regulations at 493.1256(d)(3)(i-iii), when it can demonstrate the test system's stability over time. This may be substantiated by successfully completing the evaluation process (described below).

Evaluation Process: *The laboratory must perform the test system's internal control procedure(s) in accordance with the manufacturer's instructions (but not less frequently than once each day of testing) and test two levels of external control material daily for **60** consecutive days of testing.* ***Because the test system's performance may be affected by operator variance, all personnel who will perform the test must participate in the evaluation.***

- *If the internal and external control results are acceptable throughout the evaluation process, the laboratory may reduce the frequency of testing two levels of external control material from daily to* ***once per calendar week*** *unless the manufacturer requires more frequent and/or additional external control testing*
- *[REST OF GUIDELINES ARE SAME AS FOR EARLIER OPTIONS.]*

Understanding QC Performance and Patient Safety

The purpose of QC is to detect changes in performance, i.e., changes in precision and accuracy that affect the correctness of laboratory tests. Correct test results are critical for correct patient treatment decisions. Therefore, the bottom line is that QC should protect patients from mistreatment, i.e., assure patient safety. Patient safety is the number 1 goal in healthcare today [4,5] and QC is an important part of patient safety!

In fact, safety can help us understand QC. Consider the fire alarms in public and private buildings. Fire alarms can be triggered manually or automatically, but it is the automatic mode that is now required by all building codes. The automatic mode makes use of a smoke detector, which functions very much like the error detector or QC procedure used to monitor analytical testing processes.

The smoke detector and fire alarm provide a good analogy for understanding laboratory quality control. There are many parallels.

- First of all, quality control is like safety – you do it regularly to be sure there aren't any problems, even if the historical data shows there haven't been any problems. No one argues against the required use of fire alarms and smoke detectors in public and private buildings. People safety is too important to disregard!

- Second, the smoke alarm is a fire detector, whereas QC is an error detector. Smoke and fire are related, just like errors and quality. We want to detect fire immediately to assure the safety of the people, likewise, we want to detect errors immediately to assure the safety of our patients. To do that, the detector must be carefully designed and properly implemented, e.g., smoke detectors must meet certain standards for performance, as well as being properly located and installed. Just having a smoke detector does not assure people safety! Just running controls does not assure patient safety!

- Third, the performance characteristics are similar – there may be both false alarms and true alarms. Everyone has experienced a false fire alarm and knows that it modifies their behavior when a second alarm occurs. Likewise, laboratory analysts experience false alarms, particularly when they employ 2 SD control limits, and have modified their behavior – often just repeating the controls rather than looking to see if there really is a problem.

- Concerning the other important performance characteristic – error detection, we recognize that the response of the detector will be related to the size of the fire. What size fire will be detected by your alarm system? For example, if you light one match right now, it is unlikely to set off the fire alarm. However, if you light a waste basket full of paper, there's a much higher probability the alarm will go off. What size error will be detected by a laboratory QC procedure? It shouldn't be a surprise that not all errors will be detected! But it is critical to know whether a medically important error will be detected if we are to assure patient safety. Both the smoke detector and the laboratory QC procedure need to be properly designed to have the necessary sensitivity or error detection.

If we were to test a new smoke detector according to "equivalent QC procedures," this is what we would do. Most smoke detectors would qualify for Eqc option 2 because they usually have an internal mechanism (procedural control) that allows us to manually check the alarm. That check doesn't actually test the whole analytic process because it doesn't introduce smoke, it only shorts out the detector to demonstrate that the batteries are still good and the horn still sounds. To prove that the new detector works okay, according to Eqc, we check each day for 30 days to see whether or not there is a fire (we don't actually check the detector, we just check the room). In the absence of observing a fire for 30 days and the absence of any alarms from the smoke detector, we now only need to check once a week to see if there is a fire. We trust the smoke detector will be watching out for us the rest of the time, even though we've never checked whether it will actually detect a real fire.

In the absence of any internal check for battery life and a working horn, a smoke detector would quality for Eqc option 3. That means we have to test the new smoke detector for 60 days and if we don't observe anything, then we only need to check for fire once a week. Once again, we trust that the smoke detector actually works, even though we've never tested its detection capability.

The point of this analogy is to understand that there is a need for proper design and implementation of any alarm system. Safety is not protected unless the alarm system really works. The lack of alarm signals under test conditions where there are no fires does NOT provide evidence that the alarm will detect fires. Given that proper implementation of appropriate statistical QC procedures is still a major deficiency in laboratories, the CMS evaluation protocols are critical for proving the validity of any reduction of daily QC to weekly or monthly QC.

Issues and Answers

Equivalent QC – equivalent to what?

There is no definition or discussion of the meaning of "equivalent" in the context of QC. Does it mean equivalent QC performance, i.e., the capability to detect immediate errors and monitor the precision and accuracy of the complete analytic process? That is the most obvious intent, which would mean that a scientific evaluation would be concerned with the probabilities of false rejection (false alarms) and error detection (true alarms). Does it mean equivalent quality in the outcome of the testing process? If so, a scientific evaluation would require that the quality required for the test be defined in order to assure that method performance is capable of achieving the desired level of quality under stable operating conditions and that the QC procedure is capable of detecting any instances of unstable operation. This also requires that the QC procedure be properly designed to detect medically important errors in order to alert the operator to those instances of unstable performance.

What's wrong with the CMS evaluation protocols for the Eqc options?

Eqc option 1 is for test systems with internal procedural controls that monitor the entire analytic process. How do you know the entire analytical process is being monitored? You're supposed to ask the manufacturer and trust his answer. But it is still the laboratory's responsibility to evaluate the effectiveness of the internal procedural controls. The CMS guidelines specify that the evaluation requires the laboratory to run two levels of external control daily for 10 days. If the internal and external control results are acceptable throughout the 10 day period, the laboratory may reduce the frequency of external control testing to once every 30 days. How does that work? Observing no problems in a 10 day period somehow provides evidence that there won't be any problems in a 30 day period? That conclusion requires a leap of faith and does not represent a scientific evaluation!

Eqc option 2 is intended for test systems with internal procedural controls that monitor a portion of the analytic process. The evaluation guidelines specify running two levels of external controls for 30 days. If the internal and external control results are acceptable for the 30 day period, the laboratory may reduce the frequency of external control testing to once a week. Well, at least the time dimension makes sense for this option. However, the evaluation protocol does NOT assure that the external QC procedure will detect medically important errors if they occur. How does the absence of out-of-control signals demonstrate that errors will be immediately detected when they occur? No such conclusion can be drawn – the error detection capability isn't even being tested!

Eqc option 3 is intended for test systems without any internal procedure controls. The evaluation guidelines specify testing 2 levels of external controls for 60 days. If the external controls have not identified any problems during this time period, then they need only be analyzed once a week instead of daily. Again, that conclusion cannot be made since the error detection capability isn't even tested.

What needs to be done to improve the CMS evaluation protocols?

The external QC procedures need to be carefully designed to account for the quality required by each test and the performance observed for the method in order to detect medically important errors. Unless this is properly done, the *lack of rejections* during the evaluation period cannot be taken as evidence of the *lack of problems*. For the evaluation protocols to be reliable, it would first be necessary to characterize method performance by establishing the mean and SD for the two control materials from at least 20 days of data collected in the laboratory. Then it would be necessary to select the control rules and number of control measurements that would assure detection of medically important errors, as discussed in the previous chapter. Finally, the daily operation of the control procedure requires proper interpretation of control results and should NOT allow the repeat analysis of controls in cases when a run is out-of-control. Proper design of the external QC procedure would eliminate the need for repeat analysis and assure detection of medically important errors.

Who's responsible for any decision to use Eqc procedures?

There is an important note about equivalent QC procedures in section **D5445** of the Interpretive Guidelines:

> *NOTE: Since the purpose of control testing is to detect immediate errors and monitor performance over time, increasing the interval between control testing (i.e. weekly, or monthly) will require a more extensive evaluation of patient test results when control failure occurs (see 493.1282). The director must consider the laboratory's clinical and legal responsibility for providing accurate and reliable patient test results versus the cost implications of reducing the quality control testing frequency.* [*CMS emphasis, not ours*]

The government is proposing a practice that it is not willing to condone. The laboratory can do this if the Medical Director is willing to assume the responsibility and liability. The laboratory will be in compliance with the letter of this particular law, but the government makes no guarantee about clinical or legal acceptability. Think about it: the government isn't willing to assure you that this law is clinically or even legally appropriate (a law that isn't legal?). Does that inspire confidence in you? Would that inspire confidence in the physicians and patients you serve?

Should laboratories adopt "Equivalent QC procedures"?

The Eqc options are obviously and absurdly inadequate when judged against CLIA's own standard that QC "should detect immediate errors that occur due to test system failure, adverse environmental conditions, and operator performance, monitor over time the accuracy and precision of test performance that may be influenced by changes in test system performance and environmental conditions, and variance in operator performance." The recommended evaluation protocols are also obviously and absurdly inadequate. The idea that individual laboratories rather than manufacturers can and should take responsibility for documenting the effectiveness and performance of the internal procedural controls *developed by the manufacturer* is itself absurd, particularly in light of the staffing and skill issues in laboratories today. Manufacturers are best able to do that, not individual laboratories.

Although Eqc may make it easier for a laboratory to be in *compliance* with the CLIA QC regulations, we strongly believe no laboratory should adopt the Eqc options. The goal of quality management is to satisfy patient needs for reliable laboratory tests, NOT just to be in compliance with government regulations. Compliance with the CLIA requirements in this case does not assure the quality of testing services. The goal must be to provide quality testing services! Compliance equates to being just good enough to stay out of jail. Quality is about excellence and taking proper care of our patients. The Final CLIA QC rules and Interpretive Guidelines set the standard so low that “QC” now represents only “Quality-less Compliance,” not Quality Control.

Who’s responsible for quality now?

The government is off the hook now that they’ve issued the Final CLIA Rule, and even more so because they have now said, in effect, “If these regulations aren’t clinically responsible and legally defensible, that’s not our fault, it’s the fault of the Laboratory Director and Manager who decide to follow the regulations.” Manufacturers are off the hook, having avoided the need to obtain clearance of their QC instructions, shifting rather than sharing responsibility for quality with their laboratory users and customers. The Laboratory is responsible and liable, not the manufacturer. That’s good as long as laboratories assume that responsibility with critical thought and action. It means doing the right things right, which requires knowledge and understanding of the proper way to manage the quality of laboratory testing processes.

DOs and DON’Ts

- DO be cautious and make a careful and critical assessment of the “equivalent QC procedures” before deciding to implement any of the Eqc options.
- DO check with your inspection body (CAP, JCAHO, etc) to find out their position on the Eqc options.
- DO develop more rigorous evaluation protocols that will provide adequate error detection for monitoring any tests under

consideration for Eqc. In particular, be sure to characterize the performance of the methods in your laboratory, calculate the mean and SD on control data collected in your laboratory, and calculate the control limits based on your own means and SDs, not bottle values or survey values.

- DON'T accept manufacturer's recommended protocols that include control limits or acceptability limits. Those limits will most likely represent the performance observed for a whole group of laboratories, and as such, will be too wide for a single laboratory.
- DON'T utilize manufacturer's bottle values on control materials as the acceptability limits for evaluating QC performance under the CMS evaluation protocols.
- DON'T be in any rush to implement the Eqc options. Here's a case where being first is risky. Wait and see how Eqc plays out with inspection bodies and professional organizations.

References

1. Auxter-Parham S. CLIA Interpretive Guidelines Debut on CMS Web Site: EQC options now applicable to broader spectrum of laboratory testing. Clin Lab News 2004(February issue).

2. US Centers for Medicare & Medicaid Services (CMS). Medicare, Medicaid, and CLIA Programs: Laboratory Requirements Relating to quality Systems and Certain Personnel Qualifications. Final Rule. Fed Regist Jan 24 2003;16:3640-3714.

3. CMS State Operations Manual – Interpretive Guidelines: Appendix C. www.cms.gov/clia/appendc.asp

4. Committee on Quality of Health Care in America. Institute of Medicine. To Err is Human: Building a Safer Health System. Washington DC: National Academy Press, 2001.

5. Committee on Quality of Health Care in America. Institute of Medicine. Crossing the Quality Chasm. Washington DC:National Academy Press, 2001.

15: Quality Assessment of QC Systems

The confusion over "equivalent QC procedures" reveals a fundamental lack of understanding in how to evaluate the quality of QC itself. If quality assessment is truly the interest and intent of the CLIA Final Rule [1], then it is important to develop an objective approach for the quality assessment of QC systems. There are objective planning approaches for selection of appropriate QC procedures [2], but CMS seems reluctant to implement a rigorous approach for quality assessment of QC itself.

To understand the difficulties, remember that the regulations use the term "equivalent quality testing" and CMS converts that to "equivalent QC procedures" in the Interpretive Guidelines [3]. And that's where things start to go wrong!

What's "equivalent quality"?

Let's go back to the language in the Final Rule and consider how to evaluate equivalent quality. It turns out to be rather simple. It might even make use of the evaluation data that is recommended in the original CMS guidelines, but that data needs to be analyzed in a different way to properly characterize the performance of the method in the laboratory.

To understand the problem and its solution, we must begin by understanding the meaning of the words "equivalent" and "quality."

- Equivalent implies equal – according to one dictionary "to have equal power, equal in force, amount, or value, like equal in signification or import, corresponding to or virtually identical esp. in effect or function, or equal in might or authority."
- Quality is more difficult to define, but one well-accepted definition is that quality is the "totality of features and characteristics of a product or service that bear on its ability to satisfy given needs." This definition comes from the American Society for Quality – the professionals in the field of quality. We might refine the last part of this definition – the phrase "to satisfy given needs" – to mean "to conform to the stated or implied

requirements of users and customers." That will make the definition more operative and easy to apply with existing recommendations on laboratory performance.

How do we measure "unquality"?

The difficulty with quality is how to measure it! However, as laboratory scientists who regularly deal with characteristics such as accuracy and precision, we recognize that the measures of certain characteristics are related to the "lack of" the characteristics, e.g., inaccuracy and imprecision.

- Accuracy is determined by experiments that measure the inaccuracy, as described by the bias between a method and the correct or true values (ideally obtained from a reference quality method but also by comparison with existing field methods).
- Precision is determined by experiments that measure the imprecision, as described by the SD or CV of a method.

Likewise, we should understand that the measure of quality is unquality, i.e., *the lack of conformance to requirements, which is universally described by defectives, defects, or defect rates.*

Imprecision, inaccuracy, and unquality! They're all determined by measuring the lack of agreement or the lack of conformance.

How do we define good quality?

The next step in making quality a quantitative characteristic is to define "good quality," i.e., what is needed, required, or desired. We can speak of quality in quantitative terms only when we define how good something has to be. Whether the characteristic is turnaround time or accuracy, an essential step is to define the goal or requirement, e.g., an allowable time period of 60 minutes and an allowable error of 10 mg/dL.

- A test was reported in 47 minutes. Acceptable or defective?
- A test is correct within 12.4 mg/dL. Acceptable or defective?

To manage quality, to assess it, improve it, and ultimately assure that customer needs are satisfied, it is absolutely essential to define the requirement for good quality. Otherwise, quality is only a concept, does not have any practical meaning, and will not have any impact on operations and production.

What's wrong with CMS's "equivalent QC procedures"?

Equivalent quality testing must have something to do with "testing that satisfies a defined requirement for quality." To assess equivalency, the quality that is required must be defined. Equivalent to what? Equal to what?

For analytical performance, a quality requirement can be defined in terms of an "allowable total error," such as specified in the CLIA proficiency testing criteria for acceptable performance. CLIA itself defines allowable total errors for some 80 or so tests, therefore, the CLIA regulations include minimum requirements for quality for many of the commonly performed laboratory tests.

For example, for measurements of interest in POC applications, which appears to be the main focus of the discussions in the recent news [4], CLIA defines the following allowable total errors:

- Blood gas pH should be correct within 0.04 pH Units
- Blood gas pCO_2 should be correct within 5 mm Hg
- Sodium should be correct within 4 mmol/L
- Potassium should be correct within 0.5 mmol/L
- Glucose should be correct within 6 mg/dL or 10%, whichever is greater

One might think that CMS would make use of these PT criteria for defining equivalency, but they don't. It's probably too obvious and would take away the mystery in the regulations. Truth be told, CMS doesn't know what they mean by equivalency or by quality (option 1), or if they do, they aren't telling anyone (option 2), and if they don't, they're trying to make believe they do (option 3).

If you find that confusing, that's also the nature of CMS's options for "equivalent QC procedures." The lack of clear thinking becomes obvious when you look at the "evaluation protocols," which allow a laboratory to reduce the frequency of testing external controls from daily to weekly to monthly (depending on the procedural controls included in the instrument). The evaluation process only requires the laboratory to run controls daily for 10 to 30 to 60 days (options 1, 2, and 3). The lack of any rejections during that period is taken to mean there are no defective test results, and by inference (and a great big leap of faith), that equivalent quality can be achieved by running only weekly or monthly controls.

But how can you draw any conclusion about defective results and equivalent quality if you have never defined how good a test should be? How can you detect medically important errors if you haven't defined the requirement for good quality and designed the QC procedures to detect runs with bad quality? Can you assume that simply running controls will detect any and all errors? NOT TRUE! Running controls is not the same as assessing conformance to a defined quality requirement! *That requires doing the right QC right, but the CMS recommended evaluation protocols don't!*

What's wrong with current thinking about quality?

Something is missing in current thinking about quality in healthcare today! Fundamental to the organization and operation of any business or service is the knowledge of the goals to be achieved and the requirements to be satisfied. For example, for test turnaround time, we may focus on providing 95% of our STAT testing results within one hour. For analytical quality, we may focus on providing 90% assurance that test results are correct within the CLIA allowable total errors. These goals will not be achieved without conscious efforts to plan the processes carefully, monitor performance objectively, and make improvements when necessary.

A major problem in healthcare today is that quality goals are seldom defined or even acknowledged, as evident in the CMS guidelines on equivalent quality testing and "equivalent QC procedures." Many quality programs, policies, and procedures are put in place that make it look like quality is being assessed and assured, even though the goals for good quality are never defined. How can we manage quality if we don't define how good it needs to be?

Healthcare organizations often attempt to get around this shortcoming by benchmarking performance against peer institutions. None of them have defined what good quality should be, only that they want to be as good as their competition. The result is that we often consider error rates up to 10% to be okay, 5% to be good, 1% to be excellent, and anything better than that to be fantastic.

Here's where current thinking is wrong! On the Sigma scale, 6 Sigma performance is considered the goal for world class quality and 3 Sigma performance is considered unacceptable for routine operation and production. A 10% error rate corresponds to 2.8 Sigma performance, 5% to 3.2 Sigma, and 1% to 3.8 Sigma. Instead of error rates of 10% to 1%, we need to aim for 0.1% to 0.01% to 0.001% (4.6 sigma, 5.3 Sigma, and 5.9 Sigma, respectively). *We're off by orders of magnitude in our current thinking about acceptable error rates because we haven't defined objective quality goals and therefore aren't able to assess our performance against any goals.*

Why not use Sigma metrics to evaluate quality?

When CMS says equivalent quality testing, are they asking for 3 Sigma performance or 6 Sigma performance? Will the CMS evaluation process allow laboratories to provide less than 3 Sigma performance? No one knows, but it would be easy to find out! Just apply Six Sigma concepts to "equivalent QC procedures" and evaluate method performance and the need for QC using Sigma metrics. The evaluation protocols would then focus on estimating the precision (SD or CV) and accuracy (bias) of the method, rather than assessing control status (which they can't and don't because of inadequate design). The protocols calling for 30 to 60 day evaluation would be sufficient to provide these estimates if control materials had known correct values or available peer values. It would even be okay to initially assume a bias of zero and simply estimate the precision achieved within the laboratory.

These estimates of imprecision and inaccuracy would then be used to calculate the Sigma metric for a method [Sigma = (TE_a – bias)/CV, where TE_a is the CLIA quality requirement for acceptable performance in proficiency testing]. For example, for blood pH, where TE_a is 0.040 and the observed method SD is 0.005 and bias is 0.01, Sigma would be 6.0 [(0.040-0.010)/0.005].

The QC recommendation could then be related to the demonstrated performance of the method relative to a stated quality requirement for the test. At least 6 Sigma performance should be required for all three options that allow reduction from daily to weekly or monthly QC. Any process with only 3 Sigma performance needs controls at least every shift (and methods with less than 3 Sigma performance should be replaced by better methods). Methods in-between might use daily controls.

What could be simpler?

If the goal is to provide equivalent quality testing, then CMS should modify the evaluation methodology to determine the Sigma performance of the methods and relate the QC that is needed to the performance that is demonstrated. For instruments with procedural controls, only one testing protocol is needed to obtain 30 days routine control data on two different materials. For methods without procedural controls, the 60 day protocol could be used. The CLIA criteria for acceptable performance in proficiency testing could be used as the quality goals. Sigma could be calculated for a bias of zero to make things as simple as possible. Then the recommendation for frequency of running QC could be related to the Sigma metric determined on the basis of the minimum quality required by CLIA and the actual performance observed in the laboratory.

Why not try it?

At the time of this writing, CMS is on record as saying they will evaluate data being collected in the field to assess the performance of certain instruments and methods. Let's hope they also apply the Sigma calculations as part of their evaluation before letting the SOM guidance on "equivalent QC procedures" loose in the field.

If CMS doesn't evaluate the use of Sigma metrics to assess equivalent quality, then laboratories must take responsibility to do this themselves before making any reductions in QC. Let's see if the methods are really world class and good enough to assure the safety of our patients! Let's make sure we have the data to prove our assumptions and the evidence to support our practices.

References

1. US Centers for Medicare & Medicaid Services (CMS). Medicare, Medicaid, and CLIA Programs: Laboratory Requirements Relating to quality Systems and Certain Personnel Qualifications. Final Rule. Fed Regist Jan 24 2003;16:3640-3714. 714 (available at http://www.phppo.cdc.gov/clia/pdf/CMS-2226-F.pdf)

2. Westgard JO. Internal quality control: planning and implementation. Ann Clin Biochem 2003;40:593-611. Available on the Internet at www.westgard.com/iqcpaper2003.html

3. CMS State Operations Manual – Interpretive Guidelines: Appendix C. www.cms.gov/clia/appendc.asp

4. Auxter-Parham S. CLIA interpretive guidelines debut on CMS web site: EQC options now applicable to broader spectrum of laboratory testing. Clin Lab News 2004;30:1, 8, 10.

5. Westgard JO. Six Sigma Quality Design and Control: Desirable precision and requisite QC for laboratory measurement processes. Madison WI:Westgard QC, Inc., 2001.

16: Is the Final Rule the Final Word on Quality?

Now that we've reached the final[5] release of the CLIA Final Rule and the final chapter of this book, the question undoubtedly comes to mind: Is this the final word on Quality? After a decade in the making, after all the exhaustive effort and debate, do laboratories finally have a useful set of regulations that will serve them and their customers for the foreseeable future?

It should be apparent to the reader that we are not disinterested observers of these regulations. As the CLIA regulations have emerged and evolved, we have been consistent advocates for doing what's right to manage quality, rather than accepting the minimal requirements for compliance with government regulations. We maintain that point of view in this book and have attempted to demonstrate the best way to satisfy government regulations and, at the same time, do what's right to assure laboratory test results will be reliable for patient care.

During the time the CLIA rules were evolving to the final state, laboratories (mainly) needed only to follow the manufacturer's directions, with minimal requirements to validate the performance of their methods and minimal requirements for QC to monitor ongoing method performance. The Final Rule puts more responsibility on the laboratory, less responsibility on the manufacturer, and less responsibility on the government.

In principle, this is good because professional standards of practice will be higher than the minimum regulations for compliance! In practice, we worry that laboratories today may not have the technical expertise and staffing to assume the increased responsibilities. After a decade of reductions in the education and training required for laboratory staff, in part due to CLIA's reductions in personnel standards, and now faced with serious staffing shortages, laboratories today may not have the resources needed to assume these responsibilities and implement effective quality assessment systems.

Quality or compliance?

While we may disagree with the minimalist approach for compliance, we do understand that the regulators face a difficult problem. CMS inspections still reveal there are many laboratories where there is little if any QC being done and little capability to do any better. In talking to people from CMS and CDC about the issue of "equivalent QC" and our proposal to use Sigma metrics to assess the data collected in the evaluation protocol, they have indicated it is "unrealistic" to assume that all laboratories can calculate a mean and SD! While this helps us understand the nature of the problem, we don't believe the solution is to continue to dumb down the regulations and practice guidelines. Lowering standards to increase compliance does nothing to improve and assure the quality of laboratory testing for the American public.

For many laboratories, it may be disturbing to hear that government regulations are not sufficient to provide proper guidance for their quality management practices. Cost pressures are very real today; quality pressures are mainly talk! Higher levels of institutional management often believe (accept) that compliance with government regulations is all that is necessary. This, in spite of the growing recognition that patient safety is now the #1 goal and concern in healthcare today. Quality in laboratory testing is fundamental to assuring patient safety. If laboratories don't provide correct test results, the patient is in great danger of being misdiagnosed and mistreated.

Manufacturers have a serious dilemma! They have often urged the government to reduce the regulatory requirements and, in some cases, may be directly responsible for certain amendments, such as the new "equivalent QC procedures." However, they are now finding that the quality produced by their analytical systems in the field is being limited by the technical resources and expertise in the field. For most manufacturers, whether they like it or not, their liabilities are increasing and at some point it will be necessary to support higher standards than today's minimums for compliance. Some are addressing this issue by developing improved analyzers that include improved quality systems, but such progress may actually be impeded by changes in the Final Rule. Strangely enough, the new "equivalent QC" guidelines may actually limit the use of innovative QC technology already cleared via the FDA 510K product approval process. The government's own quality system is limited by inconsistencies in the programs administered by different agencies.

We believe the road to improvement in quality and quality management practices in the clinical laboratory must begin with professional organizations, not regulatory agencies. After ten years of CLIA, it is clear that quality has not been improved by a regulatory approach. The immediate needs for improvement would best be addressed through laboratory professional organizations, e.g., CAP, CLMA, ASCP, AACC, ASCLS, etc. It is possible that ISO standards will eventually become the default standards for quality in US laboratories, but that would require they be accepted and integrated into the inspection guidelines and checklists of "deemed providers." ISO standards already supercede national government regulations in the minds of manufacturers, and they could also achieve that status in the minds of laboratorians. But that will take more time.

End of book, not end of story!

These final words were written April 1, 2004 – April Fools Day! We don't think we're being foolish in our advice and recommendations in this book, but we do recognize that the story is not yet complete. We now look forward to seeing how the Final Rule and the related Interpretive Guidelines are accepted and implemented in the real world.

We think that the actions concerning "equivalent QC procedures" will be critical and may predict the future of laboratory testing in this county. Has laboratory testing become a commodity to be regulated by the government at the lowest possible standard of practice? Or will the professional responsibilities of laboratory scientists assert a higher standard? There is clearly an opportunity to re-assert professional leadership!

The actions of CAP and JCAHO will be critical. For example, if they adopt the CMS guidelines for "equivalent QC procedures," then Eqc will become a reality. If they recommend a more rigorous qualification of systems for Eqc, then a higher standard of practice will be maintained in the many laboratories they inspect and accredit. Their decisions on Eqc will probably set the standard and direction for the future.

Other professional organizations, such as AACC, ASCP, ASCLS, CLMA, etc., also need to take a stand for quality. The scientific aspects of laboratory testing need to be affirmed, the educational and training needs must be addressed, and the business aspects of efficient organizational performance must be carefully considered. However, many current US business practices do not exemplify good conduct and adequate consideration of the public good. As healthcare organizations become more businesslike, they may be in danger of making the same mistakes.

The final word on quality?

Will laboratories embrace Eqc? That will be another benchmark and predicator of the future of laboratory medicine. As long as cost and staffing issues are paramount, there will be intense pressure to adopt any practice that reduces the effort and *apparent* cost of QC. However, no one can force you to adopt Eqc or any other practice that compromises quality care. Individuals in laboratories can insist on doing what's right for patient care, instead of accepting that compliance with regulations is good enough.

We hope that we have provided you with some of the tools to assure quality, as well as some motivation to exercise your professional responsibility. We firmly believe that doing the right thing right is the best guidance we can give you. We believe that is the answer for today's questions on compliance. Stop worrying about compliance and strive to achieve excellence. That's our best advice. What happens now with quality in your laboratory is up to you. You have the final word on quality!

Glossary of Terms

Allowable total error. An analytical quality requirement that sets a limit for both the imprecision (random error) and inaccuracy (systematic error) that are tolerable in a single measurement or single test result.

Accuracy. [NCCLS] Closeness of the agreement between the result of a measurement and the true value of the measurand. Usually expressed in the same units as the result, as the difference between the true value and the observed value, or as a percentage of the true value that the difference represents; expressed this way the quantity is more correctly termed 'inaccuracy'." Note that this represents the total error concept of accuracy because the difference between the observed value and the true value could be due to random error, systematic error, or the total error from both. The more traditional concept of accuracy has been to consider just the systematic error or "bias."

Analyte. [SOM] Means a substance or constituent for which the laboratory conducts testing. ISO uses the term measurand for the same purpose.

Analytical measurement range (AMR). [CAP] The range of analyte values that a method can directly measure on the specimen without any dilution, concentration or other pretreatment not part of the usual assay process.

Analytical run. Generally defined by CLIA as an 8 hour to 24 hour interval during which control materials must be analyzed. According to NCCLS, a run is "an interval (i.e., a period of time or series of measurements) within which the accuracy and precision of the measuring system is expected to be stable. In laboratory operations, control samples are analyzed during each analytical run to evaluate method performance, therefore the analytical run defines the interval (period of time or number of specimens) between evaluations of control results. Between quality control evaluations, events may occur causing the measurement process to be susceptible to variations that are important to detect."

Analytical sensitivity. The ability of an analytical method to detect small quantities of the measured component. Numerically characterized by determination of detection limit.

Analytical specificity. The ability of an analytical method to measure only the sought-for analyte or measurand. Numerically characterized by determination of interferences and non-specific responses to other analytes or materials.

Analytic process, system. Refers to the part of the total testing process that involves measurement and analysis, as opposed to the pre-analytic part that deals with all the steps prior to performing the test and the post-analytic part that deals with all the steps after the test result is once available.

Calibration. [SOM] Means a process of testing and adjusting an instrument or test system to establish a correlation between the measurement response and the concentration or amount of the substance that is being measured by the test procedure.

Calibration verification. [SOM] Means the assaying of materials of known concentration in the same manner as patient samples to substantiate the instrument or test system's calibration throughout the reportable range for patient test results.

Clinical reportable range (CRR). The range of analyte values that a method can measure, allowing for specimen dilution, concentration, or other pretreatment used to extend the direct analytical measurement range.

Control chart. A graphical method for displaying control results and evaluating whether a testing process is in-control or out-of-control. Control results are plotted versus time or sequential run number to display the results relative to the expected mean and control limits drawn on the chart.

Control limits. Lines drawn on a control chart to provide graphic criteria for assessing whether a measurement procedure is in-control or out-of-control. The control limits are usually calculated from the mean and standard deviation determined for a given control material. Typically control limits are drawn at the mean plus and minus 2 or 3 SDs. CAP uses the term "tolerance limits" in the General Checklist and "statistically valid acceptable range" in the Chemistry and Toxicology Checklist.

Control material. A control sample or solution that is available, often commercially, liquid or lyophilized, and packaged in aliquots that can be prepared and used individually to provide ongoing testing on a uniform and stable specimen.

Control measurement. The analytical result that is obtained when a control material is analyzed.

Control procedure, QC procedure. The protocol and materials that are necessary for an analyst to test whether the method is working properly and patient test results can be reported. A QC procedure can be described by the number of control measurements and the decision criteria (control rules) used for judging the acceptability of analytical results.

Control rule. A decision criterion for judging whether an analytical run is in-control or out-of-control. It is commonly defined by a symbol of the form A_L, where A is an abbreviation for a statistic or represents a number of control measurements, and L identifies the control limits, often specified as the mean ± a multiple of the standard deviation (s). For example:

- $\mathbf{1_{3s}}$ refers to a control rule commonly used with a Levey-Jennings chart when the control limits are set as the mean +3s and the mean -3s. A run is considered out-of-control when a single control measurement exceeds either limit.
- $\mathbf{1_{2s}}$ refers to a control rule where the control limits are set as the mean ± 2s. We recommend that 2s control limits be used only as a warning rule in a multirule type of procedure, rather than a rejection rule.
- $\mathbf{2_{2s}}$ refers to a control rule where a run is rejected when 2 consecutive measurements exceed the same mean +2s control limit or the same mean -2s control limit.

- **R_{4s}** refers to a control rule where a run is rejected when 1 control measurement in the group exceeds the mean +2s control limit and another exceeds the mean -2s control limit.
- **4_{1s}** refers to a control rule where a run is rejected when 4 consecutive control measurements exceed the same mean + 1s or the same mean -1s control limit.
- **10_x** refers to a control rule where a run is rejected when 10 consecutive control measurements fall on the same side of the mean.

Control status. Refers to the outcome of the QC process and a decision that the analytical run is "in-control", in which case patient results can be reported, or "out-of-control," in which case the patient results should be held, the problem identified and resolved, and the patient samples analyzed again.

Customer. [NCCLS] The recipient of a product or service provided by the supplier.

Deemed provider, CMS agent. [SOM] Means an entity with which CMS arranges to inspect laboratories and assess laboratory activities against CLIA requirements and may be a State survey agency, a private, nonprofit organization other than an approved accreditation organization, a component of HHS, or any other governmental component CMS approves for this purpose.

Detection limit. The smallest test value that can be distinguished from zero. Different experimental procedures give different estimates, which are called the lower limit of detection, biological limit of detection, and functional sensitivity.

Equivalent QC procedure. The term for reduced QC testing based on qualification by the prescribed evaluation protocols in the SOM. EQC procedures may allow the reduction of daily QC to weekly or even monthly QC.

Equivalent quality testing. The term in the CLIA regulations that has been interpreted by CMS in terms of equivalent QC procedures. Equivalent quality testing would seem to imply equal to a certain level of quality that must be defined.

External control material. The modifier "external" means that this material is outside the analytical system and is sampled like an individual patient specimen. The SOM makes specific mention of external control materials, even though this term doesn't appear in the Final CLIA regulations.

FDA-cleared or approved test system. [CLIA, SOM] A test system cleared or approved by the FDA through the pre-market notification (510k) or pre-market approval (PMA) process for in-vitro diagnostic use.

High complexity tests. A CLIA category of tests that has the most demanding personnel and quality requirements. Includes any tests developed by the laboratory, modified by the laboratory, or manufacturer's tests that have been classified as high complexity. Note that for QC regulations, all moderate and high complexity tests have been combined into a class called non-waived tests.

Interference. [NCCLS] Artifactual increase or decrease in apparent concentration or intensity of an analyte due to the presence of a substance that reacts nonspecifically with either the detection reagent or the signal itself.

Kit. [SOM] Means all components of a test that are packaged together.

Moderate complexity tests. A CLIA category of tests that includes about 75% of all tests performed by healthcare laboratories, including most automated analytical systems. This category has more stringent personnel requirements than for waived tests or provider performed microscopy, but less stringent personnel requirements than high complexity tests. Note that for QC regulations, all moderate and high complexity tests have been combined into a class called non-waived tests.

Multirule QC. Refers to the use of a combination of control rules for evaluation of the control results, e.g., the combination 1_{3s}/2_{2s}/R_{4s}/4_{1s}/10x is widely known and commonly referred to as the "Westgard Rules."

Non-waived tests. [SOM] Means any test system, assay, or examination that has not been found to meet the statutory criteria specified at section 353(d)(3) of the Public Health Service Act. In practice, this applies to what were formerly called moderately and highly complex tests and are now treated the same under the quality assessment regulations.

Number of control measurements. Generally refers to the number of control results that are available for inspection when assessing the control status of the analytical testing process. CLIA generally requires 2 control measurements during a 24 hour period. For certain tests, the requirement is 1 control measurement during an 8 hour period or workshift, which could mean as many as 3 during a 24 hour period.

Performance characteristic. [SOM] Means a property of a test that is used to describe its quality, e.g., accuracy, precision, analytical sensitivity, analytical specificity, reportable range, reference range, etc.

Performance specification. [SOM] Means a value or range of values for a performance characteristic, established or verified by the laboratory, that is used to describe the quality of patient test results.

Pre-analytic processes, systems. The steps in the total testing process that take place prior to the analysis of the sample. Usually considered to start with patient preparation, specimen acquisition, transport, and processing that leads to the analysis in the laboratory.

Precision. [NCCLS] The closeness of agreement between independent test results obtained under prescribed conditions. Typically described by calculating the standard deviation (s) or coefficient of variation (CV = 100*s/mean).

Post-analytic processes, systems. The steps in the total testing process that take place after the test result has been determined. Usually considers the steps in reporting test results, which may also include the interpretation of the test results.

Procedure. [NCCLS] A specified way to perform an activity.

Process. [NCCLS] One or more interrelated resources and/or activities that transform inputs (e.g., intent, policies) into outputs (eg., instruction, procedures).

Quality. [NCCLS] The totality of characteristics of an entity that bear on its ability to satisfy stated and implied needs.

Quality assessment. CLIA's term for the overall system for assuring the quality of laboratory test results. Includes the monitoring and assessment of general laboratory systems, as well as pre-analytic, analytic, and post-analytic systems, with the objective of identifying problems, making corrections, and improving the quality of testing services.

Quality assurance. [NCCLS, ISO] Planned and systematic activities to provide adequate confidence that requirements for quality will be met.

Quality management. [NCCLS, ISO] All activities of the overall management function that determine quality policy objectives and responsibilities; and implement them by means such as quality planning, quality processes, quality control, quality assessment, and quality improvement within the quality system.

Quality system. [NCCLS] The organizational structure, resources, processes, and procedures needed to implement quality management.

Random error, RE. An error that can be positive or negative, whose direction and exact magnitude cannot be exactly predicted. Described by the width of the distribution or the standard deviation (SD, s) of repeated measurements on the same sample over time.

Reference range. [SOM] Means the span of test results expected for a designated population of individuals, e.g., 95 percent of the individuals that are presumed to be healthy (or normal). Also commonly called "normal range.

Reportable range. [CLIA, SOM] The span of test result values over which the laboratory can establish or verify the accuracy of the instrument or test system measurement response.

Service. [NCCLS] The result generated by activities at the interface between the provider and the customer and by provider internal activities to meet the customer needs.

Sigma metric. A numeric value that characterize method performance in terms of the number of standard deviations or sigmas that fit within the tolerance limit or quality requirement of a test. For analytic processes, calculated as Sigma = [(%TE_a – %bias)/%CV], where TE_a is the allowable total error or CLIA PT criterion for acceptable performance, %bias represents the observed inaccuracy or systematic error of the method, and %CV represents the observed imprecision or random error of the method.

Six Sigma. A concept for world class quality and a goal for process performance that requires 6 SDs or process variation to fit within the tolerance limit or quality requirement of a process.

State Operations Manual, SOM. CMS's official document that provides guidelines for interpreting the CLIA regulations, as well as suggest probes for inspectors to use when reviewing a laboratory.

Supplier. [NCCLS] An organization that provides a product or service to the customer.

Systematic error, SE. The difference between the observed mean of the measurements and the true value is the systematic error or bias of the analytical method or test system.

Test system. [CLIA, SOM] The instructions and all of the instrumentation, equipment, reagents, and supplies needed to perform an assay or examination and generate test results.

Total error. The net or combined effect of random error (imprecision) and systematic error (inaccuracy) is the total error of the analytical method or test system.

Total testing process. CLIA's term for the entire testing process that includes pre-analytic, analytic, and post-analytic steps and procedures.

Validation. [NCCLS, ISO] Action or process of proving that a procedure, process, system, equipment, or method used works as expected and achieves the intended results.

Verification. [NCCLS, ISO] The confirmation by examination and provision of objective evidence that specified requirements have been fulfilled.

Waived tests. [SOM] Means a test system, assay, or examination that HHS has determined meets the CLIA statutory criteria for waiver under section 353(d)(3) of the Public Health Service Act.

Abbreviations

AMR	analytical measurement range.
CAP	College of American Pathologists.
CDC	Centers for Disease Control
CLIA	Clinical Laboratory Improvement Amendments of 1988
CMS	Centers for Medicare and Medicaid Services
COLA	Originally, Commission for Office Laboratory Accreditation
CRR	Clinically Reportable Range
CV	Coefficient of Variation (SD divided by mean times 100)
FDA	Food and Drug Administration
HCFA	Health Care Finance Agency
HHS	Department of Health and Human Services
ISO	International Standards Organization
JCAHO	Joint Commission for Accreditation of Healthcare Organizations
LAP	Laboratory Accreditation Program
NCCLS	National Committee for Clinical Laboratory Standards (originally)
NPT	Near Patient Testing
POC	Point Of Care
POL	Physician Office Laboratory
PPM	Provider Performed Microscopy
PT	Proficiency Testing
SD	Standard deviation, also abbreviated s
SOM	State Operations Manual
TE	Total Error

Appendix 1: Quality Requirements

Fundamental to quality control is knowing the quality that needs to be controlled. A quality requirement must be defined if the QC practice is to be rational and objective. Historically, quality control has been used in laboratories to monitor whatever quality was being achieved, not for controlling to a defined level of quality.

Analytical quality requirements

Analytical quality requirements have been defined by the CLIA-88 proficiency testing (PT) criteria for acceptable performance [Federal Register February 28, 1992;57(40):7002-7186]. These criteria are presented in three different ways:

- as absolute concentration limits, e.g., target value ± 1 mg/dL for calcium;
- as a percentage, e.g., target value ± 10% for albumin, cholesterol, and total protein;
- as the distribution of a survey group, e.g., target value ± 3 standard deviations (SD) for thyroid stimulating hormone.

In a few cases, two sets of limits are given, e.g., the glucose requirement is given as the target value ± 6 mg/dL or ± 10% (whichever is greater).

The CLIA PT criteria specify the total errors that are allowable. The total error format is implicit because the CLIA-88 rules specify that only a single test is to be performed for each PT specimen. Under such conditions, the observed analytical error will be the total error due to both inaccuracy and imprecision.

Following is a list of the CLIA proficiency testing criteria for the currently regulated analytes, based on the February 28, 1992, Federal Register.

Note: For the most up-to-date news and information on CLIA, check **http://www.westgard.com/clia.htm**

Routine Chemistry

Test or Analyte	Acceptable Performance
Alanine aminotransferase (ALT)	Target value ± 20%
Albumin	Target value ± 10%
Alkaline phosphatase	Target value ± 30%
Amylase	Target value ± 30%
Aspartate aminotransferase (AST)	Target value ± 20%
Bilirubin, total	Target value ± 0.4 mg/dL or ± 20% (greater)
Blood gas pO_2	Target value ± 3 SD
Blood gas pCO_2	Target value ± 5 mm Hg or ± 8% (greater)
Blood gas pH	Target value ± 0.04
Calcium, total	Target value ± 1.0 mg/dL
Chloride	Target value ± 5%
Cholesterol, total	Target value ± 10%
Cholesterol, high density lipoprotein	Target value ± 30%
Creatine kinase	Target value ± 30%
Creatine kinase isoenzymes	MB elevated (present or absent) or Target value ± 3 SD
Creatinine	Target value ± 0.3 mg/dL or ± 15% (greater)
Glucose	Target value ± 6 mg/dL or ± 10% (greater)
Iron, total	Target value ± 20%
Lactate dehydrogenase (LDH)	Target value ± 20%
LDH isoenzymes	LDH1/LDH2 (+ or -) or Target value ± 30%
Magnesium	Target value ± 25%
Potassium	Target value ± 0.5 mmol/L
Sodium	Target value ± 4 mmol/L
Total protein	Target value ± 10%
Triglycerides	Target value ± 25%
Urea Nitrogen	Target value ± 2 mg/dL or ± 9% (greater)
Uric acid	Target value ± 17%

Toxicology

Test or Analyte	Acceptable Performance
Alcohol, blood	Target value ± 25%
Blood lead	Target value ± 10% or ± 4 mcg/dL (greater)
Carbamazepine	Target value ± 25%
Digoxin	Target value ± 20% or 0.2 ng/mL (greater)
Ethosuximide	Target value ± 20%
Gentamicin	Target value ± 25%
Lithium	Target value ± 0.3 mmol/L or ± 20% (greater)
Phenobarbital	Target value ± 20%
Phenytoin	Target value ± 25%
Primidone	Target value ± 25%
Procainamide (and metabolite)	Target value ± 25%
Quinidine	Target value ± 25%
Theophylline	Target value ± 25%
Tobramycin	Target value ± 25%
Valproic acid	Target value ± 25%

Hematology

Test or Analyte	Acceptable Performance
Cell identification	90% or greater consensus on identification
White cell differential	Target ± 3 SD based on percentage of different types of white cells
Erythrocyte count	Target ± 6%
Hematocrit	Target ± 6%
Hemoglobin	Target ± 7%
Leukocyte count	Target ± 15%
Platelet count	Target ± 25%
Fibrinogen	Target ± 20%
Partial thromboplastin time	Target ± 15%
Prothrombin time	Target ± 15%

Endocrinology

Test or Analyte	Acceptable Performance
Cortisol	Target value ± 25%
Free thyroxine	Target value ± 3 SD
Human chorionic gonadotropin	Target value ± 3 SD or (positive or negative)
T_3 uptake	Target value ± 3 SD by method
Triiodothyronine	Target value ± 3 SD
Thyroid stimulating hormone	Target value ± 3 SD
Thyroxine	Target value ± 20% or 1.0 mcg/dL (greater)

General immunology

Test or Analyte	Acceptable Performance
Alpha-1 antitrypsin	Target value ± 3 SD
Alpha-fetoprotein	Target value ± 3 SD
Antinuclear antibody	Target value ± 2 dilution or (pos. or neg.)
Antistreptolysin O	Target value ± 2 dilution or (pos. or neg.)
Anti-Human Immunodeficiency virus	Reactive or nonreactive
Complement C3	Target value ± 3 SD
Complement C4	Target value ± 3 SD
Hepatitis (HBsAg, anti-HBc, HBeAg)	Reactive (positive) or nonreactive (negative)
IgA	Target value ± 3 SD
IgE	Target value ± 3 SD
IgG	Target value ± 25%
IgM	Target value ± 3 SD
Infectious mononucleosis	Target value ± 2 dilution or (pos. or neg.)
Rheumatoid factor	Target value ± 2 dilution or (pos. or neg.)
Rubella	Target value ± 2 dilution or (pos. or neg.)

Appendix 2: A Six Sigma Primer

While Six Sigma is the latest trend in quality management, it wasn't cut from whole cloth. Six Sigma represents the evolution of Total Quality Management with a more quantitative assessment of process performance and clearer goals for process improvement.

The principles of Six Sigma go back to Motorola's approach to TQM a decade ago. Motorola established a goal that 6 Sigmas or standard deviations of process variation should fit within the tolerance limits for the process, hence the name Six Sigma. Many of the leaders of Six Sigma, such as Harry and Schroeder [1], originally worked for Motorola.

The power of Six Sigma comes from having a universal measure of process performance on the "Sigma scale" to facilitate benchmarking across industries. The Six Sigma methodology can be applied anytime the outcome of a process can be measured. For many processes, poor outcomes can be counted as errors or defects, expressed as defects per million (DPM), then converted to a Sigma metric using a standard table available in any Six Sigma text [1]. At this time when outcomes are of great interest in healthcare, Six Sigma provides a general methodology to describe performance in quantitative terms that will be widely understood.

Two approaches for measuring process performance

Six Sigma Quality Management provides a general goal for process performance – six Sigmas of process variation should fit within the tolerance limits or quality requirement for the product. Given this goal, it is important to measure process performance to determine whether improvement is needed. There are two different methodologies. One is based on counting the defects produced by the process (an outcome measure) and the other based on measuring the variability of the process directly (a predictive measure).

The first methodology (inspect outcomes) is widely applicable in industry and healthcare and depends on counting the number of defects in the output of a process, estimating the defect rate in terms of defects per million (DPM), and then converting DPM to a Sigma metric using a standard conversion table. Whenever we estimate an error rate, we could use this methodology to convert that error rate to a Sigma metric. This first methodology is readily applicable to pre-analytic and post-analytic laboratory processes.

The second methodology (measure variation) is readily applicable to analytic testing processes and depends on being able to define the quality required for a process, measure the variation, and control the process to assure the predicted performance is actually achieved in production. We emphasize the importance of implementing the proper QC procedure to assure the method is stable and to detect any instances of instability. Unless the proper QC procedures are implemented, the predictive methodology won't provide reliable estimates of the expected Sigma performance.

A well-known industry application

A well-known tire manufacturer produced 6,000,000 tires for a particular brand of sports utility vehicle. It was reported that 2000 accidents and 100 deaths occurred due to failures of the tires. What's the performance of the production process?

Step 1. Define a defective outcome. A defect in this case is an accident. The number of deaths reflect the severity of the accidents.

Step 2. Inspect the data to determine the number of defects. In this case, there have been 2000 defects observed, according to data in the newspapers.

Step 3. Calculate the defects per million (DPM). The 2000 defects were observed in a production of 6,000,000 tires, according to the reported number of tires recalled.

- 2000/6,000,000 = 333 DPM

Step 4. Convert from DPM to a Sigma metric using a standard table from one of the Six Sigma texts. Here's a short version of such a table.

Sigma Metric	DPM without shift	DPM with 1.5s shift
1.00	317,400	697,700
2.00	45,400	308,637
2.50	12,419	158,686
3.00	2,700	66,807
3.50	465	22,750
4.00	63	6,210
4.50	6.8	1,350
5.00	0.57	233
5.50	0.038	32
6.00	0.002	3.4

- Process performance is approximately 5 Sigma using the "DPM with 1.5s shift" column, which is the standard methodology recommended in Six Sigma textbooks and training manuals. The use of column 3 for conversion is sometimes called "Sigma short term performance" in contrast to "Sigma long-term performance" which makes use of column 2 for conversion.
- *A larger version of the Sigma conversion table is provided in Appendix 3.*

Quality assessment of pre-analytic and post-analytic processes

Probably only a few processes in healthcare perform as well as Firestone tire production! You'll find that statement shocking, but error rates of 1% to 2% are often considered excellent for healthcare processes. Those error rates correspond to 10,000 to 20,000 DPM or process performance of 3.8 to 3.6 Sigma. We should be striving for error rates of 0.1% (4.6 Sigma) to 0.01% (5.2 Sigma) and ultimately 0.001% (5.9 Sigma).

The first application of Sigma metrics to laboratory data was published in 2000 by Nevalainen et al [1]. The authors utilized data from three individual laboratories, as well as summaries of performance from 300 to 500 laboratories participating in the College of American Pathologist's Q-Probe program. The original paper provides information on sample size and the number of defects or errors, which were then converted into percent errors and defects per million. DPM figures for representative quality indicators from the Q-Probe data are converted to sigma values in the table below.

Q-Probe Quality Indicator	**% Error**	**DPM**	**Sigma***
Order accuracy	1.8 %	18,000	3.60
Duplicate test orders	1.52	15,200	3.65
Wristband errors (not banded)	0.65	6,500	4.00
TDM timing errors	24.4	244,000	2.20
Hematology specimen acceptability	0.38	3,800	4.15
Chemistry specimen acceptability	0.30	3,000	4.25
Surgical pathology specimen accessioning	3.4	34,000	3.30
Cytology specimen adequacy	7.32	73,700	2.95
Laboratory proficiency testing	0.9	9,000	3.85
Surg path frozen sect diagnostic discordance	1.7	17,000	3.60
PAP smear rescreening false negatives	2.4	24,000	3.45
Reporting errors	0.0477	477	4.80

*Conversion using table with allowance for 1.5s shift

As shown for a variety of processes in this table, the approach of using outcome measures can be applied to virtually any process. The observed error rates for several of these processes are in the 3.0% to 0.3% range, which translates to typical Sigma levels of 3 to 4. Even analytical performance, as estimated from proficiency testing data, is only at the 3.85 Sigma level. The best process is "reporting errors" which has a Sigma metric of 4.80. No process achieves the Six Sigma goal. The overall average of all of these processes is 3.65 Sigma.

For comparison or benchmarking purposes, Nevalainen cited the following figures. Airline baggage handling shows a 0.4% error rate, or 4000 DPM, which is 4.15 Sigma performance. Airline safety (from the normal system of random causes, not assignable causes such as terrorist hijackings) has a very low fatality rate of 0.43 deaths per million passenger miles, which is better than the goal of

6-Sigma performance for world class quality. In industry, the minimum acceptable performance for a production process is generally set at 3.0 Sigma. Typical business processes are expected to be about 4.0 Sigma performance. As observed by Nevalainen, typical laboratory processes appear to be at the same level of typical business processes. And, as illustrated earlier, Firestone tire production is near the 5-Sigma performance level, which is better than any of the laboratory processes evaluated by Nevelainen.

Quality assessment of analytic processes

Fortunately for laboratories, it is very easy to assess the performance of analytical testing processes on the Sigma scale. The maximum tolerance limits can be taken from CLIA proficiency testing criteria; process variation and bias can be estimated from method validation experiments, peer-comparison data, proficiency testing results, and routine QC data. To calculate the Sigma metric, you can take the CLIA proficiency testing criterion, subtract the bias observed for your method, and divide by the SD or CV of your method, as shown in this equation:

$$\text{Method Sigma} = (\text{CLIA } TE_a - \text{Method bias})/\text{Method CV}$$

For cholesterol, for example, the CLIA criterion is 10%. Given a method with a bias of 0% and a CV of 2%, the process would be characterized as having 5-Sigma performance [(10-2)/2]. Given that the goal for "world class quality" is 6-Sigma performance, it follows that the goal for imprecision for a cholesterol method should be 1.7% (10/6).

By comparison, the NCEP national guidelines for cholesterol methods specify a CV of 3.0% (or better) and a bias of 3% (or better), which could lead to a process whose performance is as poor as 2.33 Sigma [(10-3)/3]. In any other industry, a process having less than 3-Sigma performance would NOT even be considered for routine production or operation. With that one example, you can see how Six Sigma impacts our thinking and understanding of process performance and changes our goals and specifications for analytical methods.

We have described the application of Sigma metrics for method validation and QC in more detail in certain chapters of this book. The method decision chart discussed in chapter 10 provides you with a practical tool for implement Sigma metrics for evaluating and validating method performance. In addition, the Sigma metrics will help you understand the QC procedures that are appropriate for methods with different Sigma performance, as discussed in chapter 13. Finally, the use of Sigma metrics will help you evaluate the new proposed "equivalent QC" options in a more objective way, as discussed in chapter 15.

Quality assessment of healthcare processes

Given the universal applicability of the Six Sigma methodology, we can expect demands by the public to know the quality of healthcare processes on the Sigma scale. If we don't make the translation, others will take the reported error rates and convert them to Sigma metrics. The public will soon have a better understanding of the quality of healthcare!

Would you like to explain to patients why healthcare processes are only as good as airline baggage handling and not even as good as Firestone tire production? The "why" is that we ourselves have not properly understood how to assess the quality of our processes and to set goals for process improvement. Six Sigma will change that forever! Laboratories are fortunate because the concepts can be easily applied and will provide a much more quantitative methodology for managing the quality of laboratory services [3].

For more detailed discussion of Six Sigma concepts and their application for establishing performance specifications and QC procedures for laboratory tests, see the following resources on Westgard Web:

- Six Sigma quality management and desirable laboratory precision. http://www.westgard.com/essay35.htm
- Six Sigma quality management and requisite laboratory QC. http://www.westgard.com/essay36.htm
- Six Sigma quality design and control processes. http://www.westgard.com/lesson67.htm

References

1. Harry M, Schroeder R. Six Sigma: The Breakthrough Management Strategy Revolutionizing the World's Top Corporations. New York:Currency, 2000.

2. Nevalainen D, Berte L, Kraft C, Leigh E, Morgan T. Evaluating laboratory performance on quality indicators with the six sigma scale. Arch Pathol Lab Med 2000;124:516-519.

3. Westgard JO. Six Sigma Quality Design and Control: Desirable precision and requisite QC for laboratory testing processes. Madison, WI:Westgard QC, Inc., 2001.

Appendix 2. Six Sigma Defects-Per-Million Table

DPM	Sigma Short Term	Sigma Long Term	Yield	Cpk
3	6	4.5	99.99966	2
5	5.9	4.4	99.99946	1.97
9	5.8	4.3	99.99915	1.93
13	5.7	4.2	99.9987	1.9
21	5.6	4.1	99.9979	1.87
32	5.5	4	99.9968	1.83
48	5.4	3.9	99.995	1.8
72	5.3	3.9	99.993	1.77
108	5.2	3.7	99.989	1.73
159	5.1	3.6	99.984	1.7
233	5	3.5	99.98	1.67
337	4.9	3.4	99.97	1.63
483	4.8	3.3	99.95	1.6
687	4.7	3.2	99.93	1.57
968	4.6	3.1	99.90	1.53
1,350	4.5	3	99.87	1.5
1,866	4.4	2.9	99.81	1.47
2,555	4.3	2.8	99.74	1.43
3,467	4.2	2.7	99.65	1.4
4.661	4.1	2.6	99.5	1.37
6,210	4	2.5	99.4	1.33
8,198	3.9	2.4	99.2	1.3
10,724	3.8	2.3	98.9	1.27
13,903	3.7	2.2	98.6	1.23
17,864	3.6	2.1	98.2	1.2
22,750	3.5	2	97.7	1.17
28,716	3.4	1.9	97.1	1.13
35,930	3.3	1.8	96.4	1.1
44,565	3.2	1.7	95.5	1.07
54,799	3.1	1.6	94.5	1.03
66,807	3	1.5	93.3	1

DPM	Sigma Short Term	Sigma Long Term	Yield	Cpk
80,757	2.9	1.4	91.9	0.97
96,801	2.8	1.3	90.3	0.93
115,070	2.7	1.2	88.5	0.9
135,666	2.6	1.1	86.4	0.87
158,655	2.5	1	84.1	0.83
184,060	2.4	0.9	81.6	0.8
211,855	2.3	0.8	78.8	0.77
241,964	2.2	0.7	75.8	0.73
274,253	2.1	0.6	72.6	0.7
308,538	2	0.5	69.1	0.67
344,578	1.9	0.4	65.5	0.63
382,089	1.8	0.3	61.8	0.6
420,740	1.7	0.2	57.9	0.57
460,172	1.6	0.1	54.0	0.53
500,000	1.5	0	50.0	0.5
539,828	1.4	-0.1	46.0	0.47
579,260	1.3	-0.2	42.1	0.43
617,911	1.2	-0.3	38.2	0.4
655,422	1.1	-0.4	34.5	0.37
691,462	1	-0.5	30.9	0.33
725,747	0.9	-0.6	27.4	0.30
758,036	0.8	-0.7	24.2	0.27
788,145	0.7	-0.8	21.2	0.23
815,940	0.6	-0.9	18.4	0.20
841,345	0.5	-1	15.9	0.17
864,334	0.4	-1.1	13.6	0.13
884,930	0.3	-1.2	11.5	0.10
903,199	0.2	-1.3	9.7	0.07
919,243	0.1	-1.4	8.1	0.03
933,193	0	-1.5	6.7	0.00